P9-BEE-446

THE WELFARE STATE

Opposing Viewpoints

THE WELFARE STATE

Opposing Viewpoints

David L. Bender

OPPOSING VIEWPOINTS SERIES

THIRD
EDITION

Greenhaven Press

577 Shoreview Park Road
St. Paul, Minnesota 55112

Third Edition
Revised and Enlarged

"Congress shall make no law...
abridging the freedom of speech,
or of the press."

first amendment to the U.S. Constitution

The basic foundation of our democracy is the first amendment guarantee of freedom of expression. The *Opposing Viewpoints Series* is dedicated to the concept of this basic freedom and the idea that it is more important to practice it than to enshrine it.

Table of Contents

Chapter 4: Are There Alternatives to Welfare?

Why Consider Opposing Viewpoints?

"It is better to debate a question without settling it than to settle a question without debating it."

Joseph Joubert (1754-1824)

The Importance of Examining Opposing Viewpoints

The purpose of this book, and the Opposing Viewpoints Series as a whole, is to confront you with alternative points of view on complex and sensitive issues.

Probably the best way to inform yourself is to analyze the positions of those who are regarded as experts and well studied on the issues. It is important to consider every variety of opinion in an attempt to determine the truth. Opinions from the mainstream of society should be examined. Also important are opinions that are considered radical, reactionary, minority or stigmatized by some other uncomplimentary label. An important lesson of history is the fact that many unpopular and even despised opinions eventually gained widespread acceptance. The opinions of Socrates, Jesus and Galileo are good examples of this.

You will approach this book with opinions of your own on the issues debated within it. To have a good grasp of your own viewpoint you must understand the arguments of those with whom you disagree. It is said that those who do not completely understand their adversary's point of view do not fully understand their own.

Perhaps the most persuasive case for considering opposing viewpoints has been presented by John Stuart Mill in his work *On Liberty*. Consider the following statements of his when studying controversial issues:

9

If all mankind minus one were of one opinion, and only one person were of the contrary opinion, mankind would be no more justified in silencing that one person than he, if he had the power, would be justified in silencing mankind...

We can never be sure that the opinion we are endeavoring to stifle is a false opinion...

All silencing of discussion is an assumption of infallibility...

Ages are no more infallible than individuals; every age having held many opinions which subsequent ages have deemed not only false but absurd; and it is as certain that many opinions now general will be rejected by future ages...

The only way in which a human being can make some approach to knowing the whole of a subject, is by hearing what can be said about it by persons of every variety of opinion, and studying all modes in which it can be looked at by every character of mind. No wise man ever acquired his wisdom in any mode but this.

Pitfalls To Avoid

A pitfall to avoid in considering alternative points of view is that of regarding your own point of view as being merely common sense and the most rational stance, and the point of view of others as being only opinion and naturally wrong. It may be that the opinion of others is correct and that yours is in error.

Another pitfall to avoid is that of closing your mind to the opinions of those whose views differ from yours. The best way to approach a dialogue is to make your primary purpose that of understanding the mind and arguments of the other person and not that of enlightening him or her with your solutions. One learns more by listening than by speaking.

It is my hope that after reading this book you will have a deeper understanding of the issues debated and will appreciate the complexity of even seemingly simple issues when good and honest people disagree. This awareness is particularly important in a democratic society such as ours, where people enter into public debate to determine the common good. People with whom you disagree should not be regarded as enemies, but rather as friends who suggest a different path to a common goal.

Analyzing Sources of Information

The Opposing Viewpoints Series uses diverse sources; magazines, journals, books, newspapers, statements and position papers from a wide range of individuals and organizations. These sources help in the development of a mindset that is open to the consideration of a variety of opinions.

The format of the Opposing Viewpoints Series should help you answer the following questions.

1. Are you aware that three of the most popular weekly news magazines, *Time*, *Newsweek*, and *U.S. News and World Report* are not totally objective accounts of the news?
2. Do you know there is no such thing as a completely objective author, book, newspaper or magazine?
3. Do you think that because a magazine or newspaper article is unsigned it is always a statement of facts rather than opinions?
4. How can you determine the point of view of newspapers and magazines?
5. When you read do you question an author's frame of reference (political persuasion, training, and life experience)?

Many people finish their formal education unable to cope with these basic questions. They have little chance to understand the social forces and issues surrounding them. Some fall easy victims to demagogues preaching solutions to problems by scapegoating minorities with conspiratorial and paranoid explanations of complex social issues.

I do not want to imply that anything is wrong with authors and publications that have a political slant or bias. All authors have a frame of reference. Readers should understand this. You should also understand that almost all writers have a point of view. An important skill in reading is to be able to locate and identify a point of view. This series gives you practice in both.

Developing Basic Reading and Thinking Skills

A number of basic skills for critical thinking are practiced in the discussion activities that appear throughout the books in the series. Some of the skills are:

Evaluating Sources of Information The ability to choose from among alternative sources the most reliable and accurate source in relation to a given subject.

Distinguishing Between Primary and Secondary Sources The ability to understand the important distinction between sources which are primary (original or eyewitness accounts) and those which are secondary (historically removed from, and based on, primary sources).

Separating Fact from Opinion The ability to make the basic distinction between factual statements (those which can be demonstrated or verified empirically) and statements of opinion (those which are beliefs or attitudes that cannot be proved).

Distinguishing Between Bias and Reason The ability to differentiate between statements of prejudice (unfavorable, preconceived judgments based on feelings instead of reason) and statements of reason (conclusions that can be clearly and logically explained or justified).

Identifying Stereotypes The ability to identify oversimlified, exaggerated descriptions (favorable or unfavorable) about people and insulting statements about racial, religious or national groups, based upon misinformation or lack of information.

Recognizing Ethnocentrism The ability to recognize attitudes or opinions that express the view that one's own race, culture, or group is inherently superior, or those attitudes that judge another race, culture, or group in terms of one's own.

It is important to consider opposing viewpoints. It is equally important to be able to critically analyze those viewpoints. The activities in this book will give you practice in mastering these thinking skills. Although the activities are helpful to the solitary reader, they are most useful when the reader can benefit from the interaction of group discussion.

Using this book, and others in the series, will help you develop basic reading and thinking skills. These skills should improve your ability to better understand what you read. You should be better able to separate fact from opinion, substance from rhetoric. You should become a better consumer of information in our media-centered culture.

A Values Orientation

Throughout the Opposing Viewpoints Series you are presented conflicting values. A good example is *American Foreign Policy*. The first chapter debates whether foreign policy should be based on the same kind of moral principles that individuals use in guiding their personal actions, or instead be based primarily on doing what best advances national interests, regardless of moral implications.

The series does not advocate a particular set of values. Quite the contrary! The very nature of the series leaves it to you, the reader, to formulate the values orientation that you find most suitable. My purpose, as editor of the series, is to see that this is made possible by offering a wide range of viewpoints which are fairly presented.

David L. Bender
Opposing Viewpoints Series Editor

Introduction: The Dilemma of Welfare

> *"It is perfectly true that that government is best which governs least. It is equally true that that government is best which provides most."*
>
> Walter Lippman, *A Preface to Politics*

When Franklin D. Roosevelt was elected president in 1932, the United States was in the midst of the Great Depression. An aura of despair enveloped the country as chronic unemployment, large and small business failures and the collapse of countless savings institutions spread with epidemic swiftness and virulence. The economic situation kept plummeting downward creating a vicious cycle. As more and more businesses failed or declined, the ranks of the unemployed and needy grew. To combat the menace and provide a psychological bolster to a disheartened nation, Roosevelt, in his inaugural address, offered his fellow citizens a "New Deal." The "New Deal" was to do more than revitalize the sick economy. It promised to infuse the entire economic system with a social conscience.

"The money changers," he said, "have fled from their high seats in the temple of our civilization. We may now restore that temple to the ancient truths. The measure of the restoration lies in the extent to which we apply social values more noble than mere monetary profit." Roosevelt subsequently converted these words into deeds by successfully guiding through Congress a host of economic and social welfare legislation. This legislation not only succeeded in providing employment and other forms of economic relief, but it also set in motion an innovative and irreversible trend in American society. By using federal or public funds to finance the welfare needs of the people, the government was involving itself in areas which previously were the preserve of the private sector of the economy.

At the time of Roosevelt's first administration, the theory and practice of welfare were not new in the United States. Greatly influenced by European reformers, many Americans, toward the end of the nineteenth century, were providing relief to

13

unemployed and low income families in slum and devastated areas throughout the country. Jane Addams' Hull House in Chicago, the Salvation Army, and the American Red Cross were just some of the numerous agencies dedicated to this task. Even Andrew Carnegie, America's premiere industrialist and defender of the capitalistic system, believed it was his duty to channel many of his millions into charitable foundations. Yet the "New Deal" took America beyond these earlier instances of private philanthropy. For the first time on so large a scale, the government took it upon itself to oversee the welfare needs of the country. By way of government dole or subsidized work projects, every taxpayer, like it or not, was contributing to the economic relief of the nation's needy.

Many claimed that the "New Deal" was cutting into the very heart of the free enterprise system in the United States. They saw it as a form of "creeping socialism" which, in time, would totally undermine the work ethic crucial to the success of capitalism. The end result would be the establishment of a "Welfare State" in which most or all social and economic services would be dealt with by the government. However, supporters of the "New Deal" were convinced that there was no alternative. Private funds were obviously not relieving the economic plight of the nation and therefore it was the moral duty of government to act decisively.

With the arrival of World War II and the general prosperity which followed it, the "New Deal" was laid to rest. Yet the debate regarding Welfarism continues and, indeed, has broadened. The Welfare State and its underlying philosophy is still being attacked by conservative politicians and by countless economic, political and social commentators. Critics now maintain that the system has been tried and allege that its failures are glaring. They point to the impending bankruptcy of the Social Security system, the growing number of welfare recipients and the existence of an unwieldy and costly welfare bureaucracy as just some examples of these failures. And, according to many, while welfare was created to ultimately relieve unemployment and indigence, it has been largely responsible for creating a permanent jobless class. Defenders of the system contend that the philosophical foundations of welfare have always been and still remain morally, socially and economically sound. Recognizing that defects in the system do exist, most, they feel, are not beyond remedy. Moreover, where defects cannot be repaired, compatible alternatives are available.

This anthology of Opposing Viewpoints attempts to present the reader with a wide range of arguments reflecting the positions outlined above. Although it is a revision of an earlier work (*Liberals and Conservatives: A Debate on the Welfare State,*

1973), it has been considerably enlarged, both topically and in length, and contains eighteen new viewpoints. In the editor's opinion, it offers a cross-section of many of the more relevant contemporary and timeless arguments regarding the Welfare State. The topics debated include: Does the Welfare State Benefit Society?, Should the Welfare System Be Reformed?, What Is the Role of Social Security? and Are There Alternatives to Welfare? To aid the reader, the following two pages contain a list of brief arguments *for* and *against* the Welfare State. The editor believes that this list will provide a frame of reference helpful in evaluating the ensuing debates.

Arguments For the Welfare State

1. Economic equality is the foundation on which basic freedoms rest. The welfare state can insure a basic economic equality for everyone.

2. Society has a moral responsibility to provide a minimum subsistence level for those citizens who are not able to provide it for themselves.

3. The welfare state represents a "compromise system" midway between an authoritarian government that satisfies everyone's minimum economic needs and a capitalistic system that leaves this task solely to the individual's initiative and ability.

4. Many western democracies have already developed an advanced welfare state. The march of history indicates it is inevitable that the United States also expand its welfare programs.

5. The continued economic growth of the United States' economy is dependent on an expanded welfare economy. The welfare state makes consumers out of individuals who would otherwise make no contributions to our economy.

6. The sickness of any member of a society will adversely affect the whole society. For this reason, it is in society's best interests to help individuals in need of assistance.

7. To ask for and receive charity is a degrading psychological experience. It is better for individuals to receive help through a government insurance program in a more anonymous fashion.

8. Our technological society, which finds millions of citizens dependent on large corporations and economic conditions beyond their control for their livelihood, should provide financial assistance when people find themselves victimized by the system through unemployment, expensive hospital care, nursing homes that few people can afford, etc.

Arguments Against the Welfare State

1. The government has no right to give away the tax dollars of hard working people to those who are unable or unwilling to work.

2. Individual citizen's qualities of initiative and ambition will be destroyed in a "something for nothing society."

3. Local governments and private charities are better able to resolve welfare problems because of their nearness to these problems. The federal government is too distant and impersonal.

4. The welfare state may destroy the capitalistic system which has made America rich and powerful and the land of opportunity for millions of immigrants.

5. The welfare state is incompatible with democracy and may lead to socialism or communism or some other form of totalitarian government.

6. The welfare state will foster an immense bureaucratic monster that will be buried in its own red tape.

7. Not only will the welfare state bring about a loss of personal responsibility and individual initiative, it will also do psychological harm when large numbers of people suffer a lack of pride in accomplishment because of work they have not done.

8. The welfare state will dispense aid and assistance in an impersonal and bureaucratic manner. It is preferable that people receive help from private charities on a person to person basis.

9. Welfare programs, once established, will be difficult to remove, even though they prove to be ineffective and perhaps harmful to our society.

Does the Welfare State Benefit Society?

"A government which has secured the greatest degree of welfare for its people is the government which stands most firmly against totalitarianism."

The Welfare State Promotes Freedom

Herbert H. Lehman

Herbert H. Lehman was governor of New York from 1932-1942 and a U.S. senator from 1949-1956. A "New Deal" democrat, he was one of the most prominent and influential figures in the Democratic Party in the United States before his death in 1963. In the following viewpoint, Governor Lehman contends that true freedom can only be realized when people are at liberty "to develop their individual capacities" and that this can only occur in a state where there is freedom from want. Although the viewpoint is taken from an address presented by him in April, 1950 before the League for Industrial Democracy, it embraces timeless principles which supporters of the welfare state still echo today.

Consider the following questions while reading:

1. What does Senator Lehman feel is the essential and basic program of the welfare state?
2. Why does the author feel that the welfare state is a good defense against totalitarianism?

Herbert H. Lehman, "Freedom and the General Welfare," *Freedom and the Welfare State*, (New York: League for Industrial Democracy, 1950). Reprinted with permission from the League for Industrial Democracy.

It has become fashionable in circles of political reaction to attack the concept of the welfare state as being prejudicial to individual liberty and freedom. These reactionaries view with fright and alarm the current and proposed activities of government in the fields of housing, health, and social security.

Cries of the Alarmists

"These are steps on the road to Communism," the alarmists cry. But these same men uttered the same cries in the same tones of fear and outrage when President Roosevelt proposed the Securities and Exchange Act, the Fair Labor Standards Act, the Holding Company Act, the Federal Deposit Insurance Act and many other pieces of legislation which even reactionaries would not dare to attack today. The same cries were raised when Woodrow Wilson proposed the Federal Trade Commission Act in 1913 and when the Railway Labor Act was first placed on the statute books in 1926. I could cite laws and programs by the score enacted over the violent opposition of the reactionaries — laws and programs which were assailed as communistic at the time — but which are now accepted even in the most conservative circles.

This cry of state tyranny has been raised during the last half century whenever the community has attempted to interfere with the right of a few to destroy forests, exploit little children, operate unsanitary and unsafe shops, indulge in racial or religious discrimination, and pursue other policies endangering the health, safety and welfare of the community. These few have completely ignored the fact that, when their license to exploit the community was restricted, the freedom of the many from ignorance, insecurity, and want — the freedom of the many to live the good life — was measurably enhanced.

Social Welfare vs. Special Privilege

I do not believe that our Federal government should seek to assume functions which properly belong to the individual or to the family, to the local community, or to free organizations of individuals. But I do believe that our Federal government should and must perform those functions which, in this complex and interdependent society, the individual, the family, or the community cannot practicably perform for themselves.

Today we in America and in the entire freedom-loving world are confronted with a world-wide threat to that principle which we hold most dear, the principle of individual dignity and of individual freedom. For the preservation of that principle we are willing to dedicate our lives, if it should prove necessary. But while this is a threat which we face on the world front, we face another danger here at home. That is the threat to our freedom from those within our country who would identify individual freedom with special privilege. Any move to diminish privilege, to stamp out discrimination and to bring security to our citizens is branded by these peoples as un-American.

Not so long ago an American political leader said that "the governments of the past could fairly be characterized as devices for maintaining in perpetuity the place and position of certain privileged classes. The government of the United States, on the other hand, is a device for maintaining in perpetuity the rights of the people, with the ultimate extinction of all privileged classes." Was it some Communist, some irresponsible radical or reformer, who made that statement? No, it was not. It was the late President Calvin Coolidge in a speech at Philadelphia in 1924.

It is my firm belief that the extinction of special privilege is an essential and basic program of the welfare state. Today the forces of special privilege provide the chief opposition and raise the wildest cries of alarm against economic security for all.

Welfare State a Foe of Totalitarianism

In addition to the forces of special privilege who are opposed, on principle, to all social legislation, there are some

IF YA GOT SOMETHIN' IT'S CAUSE YOU'RE GOOD
IF YA GOT NOTHIN' IT'S CAUSE YOU'RE BAD...
ASK SANTA CLAUS

©1968 R.COBB ALL RIGHTS RESERVED

Reprinted with permission of Sawyer Press, L.A., CA.

who, while paying lip service to liberalism, claim to be troubled by the expanding scope of government in its direct concern with the welfare of the individual citizen. These people, while conceding merit to the specific programs of the welfare state, and while approving the welfare state programs of the past, join with the forces of privilege in contending that if the government provides any further services, it is moving in the direction of totalitarianism.

In my opinion these men of little vision have lost sight of the most important — and to me the most obvious — truth of our times — that a government which has secured the greatest degree of welfare for its people is the government which stands most firmly against totalitarianism. The critics of the welfare state do not understand this simple fact. They spend their time looking for Communists in and out of government and at the same time attack those measures which would deprive Communists and would-be Communists of their ammunition — and of their audience. The measures which would provide for the welfare of the people are the surest weapons against totalitarianism.

The Communist international, its leaders, and their philosophy, have been responsible for many designs which we in the democratic world consider the quintessence of evil. Certainly the suppression of basic rights — the police state and the slave labor camp — constitutes the most repulsive and obnoxious way of life we can imagine.

But, as a liberal, I have a *special* resentment against the Communists. I feel that one of their greatest disservices to the cause of human progress has been their identification of economic security with the suppression of freedom. It is their claim that in order to achieve the solution of the economic needs of the many, it is necessary to curb the freedoms of all. They say, in effect, that you cannot have a full stomach and a free mind at the same time.

I reject this concept! I reject it as being the ultimate in reaction. This is but another demonstration of the basic affinity between Communists and reactionaries in their thinking about man and his problems. *Both* groups believe that a nation of free men cannot possibly conquer the scourges of hunger, disease, lack of shelter, intolerance and ignorance. And they *both* have much to gain if they convince enough people that freedom and security are incompatible.

Insecurity a Threat to Freedom

It is a strange paradox that the same conservatives and reactionaries who pose as champions of national security express the greatest antagonism toward individual security. Most of us readily acknowledge that the nations of the world cannot be free if they are not secure. It seems equally logical to me that *individuals* cannot be free if they are beset by fear and insecurity. To my mind the welfare state is simply a state in which people are free to develop their individual capacities, to receive just awards for their talents and to engage in the pursuit of happiness, unburdened by fear of actual hunger, actual homelessness or oppression by reason of race, creed or color.

The fear of old age, the fear of sickness, the fear of unemployment, and the fear of homelessness are not — as some would have us believe — essential drives in a productive society. These fears are not necessary to make free competitive enterprise work. The fear of insecurity is rather a cancer upon free competitive enterprise. It is the greatest threat which confronts our economic system. I hasten to add that I believe in free competitive enterprise. I believe it is the best system yet devised by man. But it is not a goal in itself. It must always serve the public interest...

We are still far from the goal we seek. Insecurity still haunts millions. Inadequate housing poisons the wells of family life in vast numbers of cases. Inadequate schooling handicaps a great segment of our people. And the fear of sickness and old age still clutches at the hearts of many if not most of our fellow citizens. Until we solve all these problems and quiet all these fears, our people will not be truly free.

"The welfare state kills political freedom and economic incentive."

The Welfare State Destroys Freedom

Ruth Alexander

A former lecturer and columnist (now retired), Ruth Alexander received a Ph.D. in journalism from Northwestern University (1932). During her career, she held several positions in journalism including associate editor of *Finance* magazine and editorial columnist for the defunct *New York Mirror*. Dr. Alexander is a member of the Authors Guild of the Smithsonian Institute. In the following viewpoint, she offers a stinging condemnation of the welfare state. After presenting several reasons for her condemnation, Dr. Alexander concludes by writing that while welfarism begins by protecting people, it ends by destroying them.

Consider the following questions while reading:
1. What does the author see as the primary consequence of the welfare state?
2. How does Dr. Alexander see the welfare state as being opposed to constitutional government?
3. Why does the author claim that "poverty is the best policy" under the welfare state?

Dr. Ruth Alexander, "What Price the Welfare State?," *Vital Speeches of the Day*, January 15, 1952. Reprinted by permission of *Vital Speeches*.

The common denominator of all Welfare States, which vary in degree but not in kind, is that the seat of authority is vested in the State — not in the citizens. It is not government OF or BY the people but OVER the people. The State is the Master, and THE people become ITS people — subjects of all-powerful, self-perpetuating government. Voting may continue but is reduced to a mere formality, as political favoritism progressively determines the outcome of elections.

In its early stages, the Welfare State governs by 'emergency decrees.' But gradually, as emergencies occur again and again, they reveal themselves to have been designed for keeps. Their purpose was to transfer power from the people to the State. For socialism regards revolution as a means to the end — POWER. Its cynical humanitarianism that "the end justifies the means" implies that it is based on an heroic redress of economic wrongs. But social gains are incidental...

Government by Man, Not Law

A primary consequence of the Welfare State is, therefore, Executive Government. Government by a Man — or Men. Not government by Law. It does not exist to serve the general welfare but to serve the welfare of special interests in return for political support. It obstructs the general welfare on behalf of these selective groups by its planned economy, especially by its managed money. Labor and the farmers, called in Europe Workers and Peasants, and those who are unable or unwilling to produce what they must, of necessity, consume, are the beneficiaries of Welfare State economy.

In the United States, organized labor has been given preferential treatment in the courts and has been absolved from anti-trust laws. In cases where the escalator clause was part of the wage agreement, labor was further provided with a hedge against inflation. This resulted in an unfair advantage over management, but it assured labor's political support. Similarly, the farmers were guaranteed relative immunity from inflation device of parity prices. Thus a favorable farm vote was also assured.

Constitutional government, on the other hand, exists to promote the general welfare, as enjoined by the Founders of this Republic. It is government by law — not men — and rests on the greatest good to the greatest number. To economic Man, this means the greatest quantity and the highest quality of goods and services at the lowest price to the greatest number. To political Man, it means the highest degree of freedom compatible with organized society. To spiritual Man, it means the quality of mercy between man and his brother-man — a quality that is inconceivable between the remote impersonal State and the victims of its mass charity.

26

Our Golden Rule declares that we must share one another's burdens on a voluntary basis. But it does not demand compulsory charity on a conveyor-belt basis. We all recognize that the mentally and physically sick and the helpless aged must be cared for by their neighbors, if they or their families are unable or unwilling to care for them. But we can, and always have, cared for them at local levels where human distress could not be exploited for political purposes. Under the 'Welfare' State, misery is for sale and the price is a vote...

In short, constitutional government aims at progressive extension of individual liberty as the sole basis for human happiness. It is the real revolutionary, the true progressive, opposed to the retrogressive Welfare State that would take us backward down the long dark road from freedom to bondage — bondage to the so-called 'social whole.'

The economic outline of the Welfare State is as follows. If you work hard and save part of what you earn, you will have to support others. If you don't, they will have to support you. The inescapable conclusion is, therefore, that POVERTY IS THE BEST POLICY...

Universal equality of goods and services is the avowed aim of the Welfare State. Those at the bottom know they cannot reach the top. So they delight in bringing the top down to their level.

Perverted Equality

The Welfare State subscribes to this primitive and perverted interpretation of equality instead of equality before law. It reverses the role of privilege. Under its aegis, those who produce and exchange our goods and services are the under-privileged classes. They are helpless before the progressive plunder of their earnings and their savings by the State...

In contrast to the harassed and underprivileged creators of our national wealth are the beneficiaries of the Welfare State. They are the newly privileged classes. Like the aristocrats of old, these modern Princes of Privilege can enforce their demands that others support them. Nobody knows whether their dependent status was brought about through misfortune, evil doing, or intent. And nobody cares — as long as they deliver the votes.

Price is Slavery

As time goes on, they claim a right to everything for which they feel a need or which they see their neighbors enjoy. Content to begin at subsistence level, social workers soon make them discontent. Food, clothing and shelter is soon discarded for demands for kinds of each. Quality, not quantity, becomes their cry, as they are excited by professional reformers who tell them that their lot is undeserved; that it is somebody else's fault; that society 'owes' them a living. What they owe to society is conveniently omitted. And nobody reminds these Welfare beneficiaries that the price of privilege is slavery.

Constitutional government is limited to guaranteeing every citizen the right to pursue happiness. But Welfare government guarantees the possession of happiness as well, in return for political support...

Capitalism has done more to eradicate poverty by the simple system of rewarding success and punishing failure, than any other system known to Mankind. Capitalism inherited poverty from its predecessor, the Welfare State of feudal socialism. It did not 'create' poverty. On the contrary, CAPITALISM CREATED WEALTH. It is the great Humanitarian of History for it freed man from bench labor — it gave him leisure and translated the luxuries of former days into the necessities of today...

In short, the Welfare State kills political freedom and economic incentive. It begins slowly by controlling things. It ends by controlling US. It begins by proclaiming Government as our Guardian. It ends by establishing Government as our Master. It begins by 'protecting' MEN. It ends by destroying MAN.

"We can learn lessons from Sweden, including the value of preventive social policy as more humane, efficient, and effective."

The Positive Side of Sweden's Welfare

Allan C. Carlson

Allan C. Carlson received his Ph.D. in European History from Ohio University. The author of numerous articles for journals such as *Public Interest* and *Policy Review*, he wrote the following viewpoint while serving as Assistant Director of the Office for Governmental Affairs of the Lutheran Council in the USA. In it, he maintains that Sweden's welfare system "tends to reduce levels of suffering, raise human dignity and preserve social harmony."

Consider the following questions while reading:
1. According to Mr. Carlson, in what way does the American view of welfare problems differ from that of the "welfare states"?
2. What are the major components of Sweden's comprehensive social policy the author describes?
3. What are the negative aspects of Sweden's policy the author mentions and what lessons can America learn from those negative aspects?

Americans tend to view the welfare problem from a "symptom-oriented" perspective; we deal with each problem or need separately, as we become aware of it...

Comprehensive Social Policies

The "welfare states" of Sweden, Norway, Denmark, and Great Britain, while politically and culturally similar to the USA, have oriented their social policies toward prevention. Assuming that the prevention of social problems is more efficient and economical than remedial actions, these nations have committed themselves to a comprehensive social policy funded largely through the tax system and covering *all* their citizens, not just the poor or those unemployed.

The complete welfare state involves a high degree of governmental planning and the tight regulation of consumption patterns. It means greater "vertical" income redistribution from the rich to the poor and disabled. It requires "horizontal" redistribution between families with children and single or childless persons. An individual pays out more during periods of relative financial abundance (for example, persons in the 45-65 age category) and receives more benefits during periods of need (years of education, family rearing, old age, times of unemployment).

The welfare state necessitates a high degree of collective responsibility for children, the elderly, the disadvantaged, and the handicapped. The government closely coordinates social policies with economic planning, the regulation of private industry and voluntary organizations, and a commitment to full employment.

The Swedish system is usually cited as the model for the modern, democratic welfare state. Major components of its comprehensive social policy are:

Employment. The Swedish government assumes that employment for everyone seeking work represents the most effective form of preventive social policy. Full employment increases self-esteem, places persons in productive rather than dependent positions, and generates income rather than expenses for the national treasury. Sweden's commitment to this policy is implemented through vocational training and guidance programs, relocation grants, extensive governmental control of industrial planning to maintain production levels, and the creation of a reserve of needed public works projects for periods of economic stress.

Families. Building on reforms first implemented in the 1930s to encourage family formation and remove the social and economic impediments to rearing children, Sweden's family policy seeks to reconcile family life with modern industrial society. Low-interest loans are available to newly married

31

couples. Pre- and postnatal maternal care and childbirth costs are fully assumed by the state insurance program. All new parents are eligible for an allowance for up to seven months, payable to the parent staying at home. Working parents are also entitled to allowances and paid leave for the special care of children...

Housing. In addition to rental allowances for families, such support is also provided to persons with low incomes, the handicapped, and elderly.

Health care. All Swedes and resident foreigners are covered upon registration by the national health insurance program. Visits to doctors, house calls, telephone consultations, hospital care, and pharmaceutical benefits are provided at nominal fees controlled by the government, with the insurance system covering the bulk of the cost. Allowances are paid to persons who cannot work because of illness. Basic vaccinations are free. Adults are covered by a national dental insurance plan.

Social insurance. Pension programs are established for the elderly, disabled, widowed, orphaned, and handicapped. Industrial injuries insurance includes sickness, disability, and death benefits.

The Conscience of a Nation

The trend in Sweden has been towards a steadily increasing responsibility on the part of the community for the social security of its citizens, and for the provision of increased social services.

Ake Fors, *Social Policy and How It Works*, published by the Swedish Institute.

These programs represent only a partial list of the services provided by the Swedish welfare state. Also in the picture are subsidized transportation, aid and employment opportunities for the handicapped and retarded, low cost day-care centers, sex education programs, annual four-week paid vacations for all workers, home nursing care, state subsidized homes for the aged, grants for holidays for housewives, grants to adapt homes for the handicapped, low cost public law offices, day centers, domestic help and even pedicure services for the elderly, student benefits, and funeral grants.

Both Advantages and Disadvantages

Advantages and disadvantages of the system are clear. It provides a guaranteed minimum level of income and security for all Swedish citizens. It insures a high degree of equity among persons in various social and economic classes in basic health and educational services. It means close scrutiny of quality and cost. It tends to reduce levels of suffering, raise

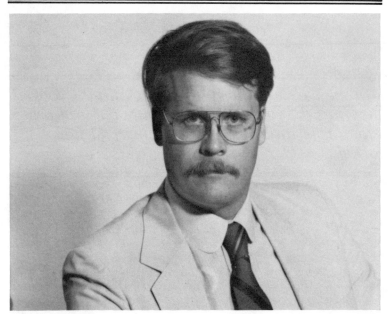
Allan C. Carlson

human dignity, and preserve social harmony...

Negative aspects are also apparent. Taxes, raised primarily through income and sales levies, are the Western world's highest, taking over 50% of the average worker's income. The income tax's progressive nature tends to discourage extra effort or innovation by taxing up to 90% of incremental income increases among moderate income workers.

With so much national income absorbed by the state, government bureaucracies wield considerable power and have often proved rigid, arrogant, and stifling. Voluntary activities in the educational, health, and welfare areas tend to fall under governmental domination or disappear altogether...

Yet we can learn lessons from Sweden, including the value of preventive social policy as more humane, efficient, and effective; the need for a greater sense of community responsibility for social problems and persons needing help; awareness of the components of an effective family policy; and the long-term political importance of universal coverage.

We can also learn from the negative side of the welfare state and seek to temper and restrain the excesses of bureaucracy and recognize the need to protect incentives for personal initiative and responsibility.

Basing welfare reform measures on such adaptations would work to the advantage of all Americans.

"In the welfare states...'commercialism' is looked upon as the root of all evil...(but) the welfare state...is virtually the most commercial state of all."

The Negative Side of Sweden's Welfare

Sven Rydenfelt

Sven Rydenfelt is professor of economics at the University of Lund, Sweden. In the following viewpoint, he contrasts the welfare systems of Sweden and Japan and suggests that the Swedish system is socially and morally inferior to the Japanese. The contrast is revealing inasmuch as the Swedish state employs public welfare while Japan relies upon family-centered private welfare.

Consider the following questions while reading:

1. How does the author test the "dogma" that the welfare of a nation's people "can't be secured without extensive public intervention?"
2. In the author's opinion, how do the Swedish and Japanese welfare states differ?
3. What does the author mean by "hired love?"

Sven Rydenfelt, "The Swedish and Japanese Welfare States." Reprinted by permission of *The Wall Street Journal,* © Dow Jones & Company, Inc., September 30, 1981. All Rights Reserved.

In current language a welfare state means a state where the care of dependent members — young, sick, handicapped, unemployed, aged — is mostly performed by public agencies.

We tend to forget, however, that virtually all societies are welfare states, whose weak members are taken care of, usually within the family group. In cases where the families for some reasons are unable to take care of their members, other people — friends, relatives, benefactors, charitable funds and societies — are usually prepared to lend a helping hand. In typical welfare states like Sweden the politicians, however, want a monopoly on charity and systematically try to kill incentives to private charity by refusing tax exemptions.

Sweden vs. Japan

In the welfare states there developed a strong conviction that the welfare of the citizen — health and longevity — can't be secured without extensive public intervention. This conviction soon became dogma.

In order to test this dogma, we have to compare the welfare achievements of different systems, comparisons which cannot be done without establishing criteria for welfare standards. According to the World Health Organization (WHO) *mean life expectation* and *infant mortality* may be used as means of measurement. These criteria can be used to compare the performance of Sweden and Japan, two typical welfare states — Sweden an outstanding representative of the public welfare system and Japan a good representative of the family-centered private welfare system. The latest available data are presented in the following tables:

Mean Life Expectancy From Birth In Years

	1960	1970	1979
Sweden	73.5	74.5	75.6
Japan	67.9	72.5	76.2

Deaths During the First Year Per 1,000 Live Births

	1960	1970	1979
Sweden	16.6	11.0	7.5
Japan	33.8	12.6	8.0

Sources for both tables: National Central Bureau of Statistics (Sweden) and Ministry of Health and Welfare (Japan).

From the tables it is apparent that Japan, starting from a welfare situation much worse than that in Sweden, has continually advanced and in 1979 caught up with Sweden as for longevity and very nearly as for infant mortality. It must also be remembered that the Swedish figures are unique in the world;

the U.S., for example, lags behind Sweden and Japan in both categories.

In the Swedish mass media there have been numerous reports about the Japanese economic "miracle." These reports are difficult for welfare state citizens to digest, fed up as they are with the dogma of the total superiority of the public welfare system. As a consolation and a support for faltering Swedish self-confidence the reports are, as a rule, concluded by a litany about the deplorable situation of old people in Japan, people who lack state pensions and, therefore — according to the welfare state ideology — must live in misery and squalor.

As demonstrated in the tables, however, this is evidently a myth, a myth the Swedes evidently need and, therefore, cling to. If the myth had been true, mortality among old people in Japan would have been higher and life expectancy lower.

The Japanese Example

In Japan, people obviously have been able successfully to adapt to life conditions in a state with little public welfare. They save extensively during their active years, and thus are able to enjoy the good life even in old age. Whenever required, their children and relatives are prepared to support them. Such longevity is achieved despite housing standards which are substantially lower than in Sweden. Obviously these low standards are compensated for by other favorable factors, among them a warmer emotional climate.

In Japanese families, mothers, as a rule, leave the labor force and remain at home as soon as the first baby is born. Most of them stay at home for the rest of their lives. When the children have grown up and left home, the mothers very often take care of aged parents.

In industry and trade, the human relations between employers and employees are much better than in Sweden. Employment is often like a lifelong marriage with strong feelings of loyalty and responsibility between the parties. These feelings function as fuel for fantastic working performances. The contrast to Sweden with its animosity and bitter confrontations in the labor market is striking.

In these intimate human relations, affection and love are normal ingredients. Children feel wanted and needed, and gain a sense of self-confidence and dignity lasting for life. And according to modern medical science concerning psychosomatic relations, such an emotional climate can only be good for health and longevity.

"Hired Love"

In the welfare states — as well as in the socialist states — "commercialism" is looked upon as the root of all evil, especially in such typical public welfare areas as education, medicine, housing and culture. And, of course, street prostitution — "hired love" — is looked upon as the worst of all. But the welfare state system is fundamentally based on "hired love." After a year of staying home with baby (during which they continue to receive wages) Swedish mothers normally rejoin the labor force and leave their babies to day-nurseries or in family day-care homes. In either case, what the child receives is "hired love."

"1984" Revisited

A visiting journalist once described Sweden as "a totalitarian state masquerading as a democracy..." As far as I am concerned the Sweden experiment is too close to "1984" and "Brave New World" for comfort.

Roland Huntford, *The Observer*, London.

In their old age, people are taken care of in their homes as long as possible by "home Samaritans," employed by local governments — again, "hired love." When, finally, they can no longer manage in their homes they are moved into "homes for the aged" and taken care of by the staff — "hired love."

In spite of the offical repudiation of street prostitution and "hired love," the welfare state is fundamentally based on the dogma that in child care, education, sick care and old-age care, commercially "hired love" is as good as love given and taken without payment between persons with intimate human relations. The welfare state, with "hired love" as one of the cornerstones, is virtually the most commercial state of all. And the strength of that stone must be decisive for the solidity of the building.

Distinguishing Between Fact and Opinion

When investigating controversial issues, it is important that one be able to distinguish between statements of fact and statements of opinion.

This activity is designed to help develop the basic reading and thinking skill of distinguishing between fact and opinion. Consider the following statement as an example. "Under a public welfare system, the government establishes and pays for entitlement programs for various members of society." This statement is a fact which no citizen of any political persuasion would deny. But consider a statement which deals with the morality of public welfare. "The government has the moral obligation to provide welfare benefits to those who cannot provide for themselves." Such a statement is clearly an expressed opinion. Whether or not one believes that it is the duty of government to provide directly for the welfare of needy citizens *will* depend upon one's political persuasion. There are those who believe that welfare undermines the economic and moral growth of a nation. Conversely, there are those who believe that to deny welfare to the needy will contribute to the moral decay of a nation.

Most of the following statements are taken from the viewpoints in this chapter. The rest are taken from other sources. Consider each statement carefully. *Mark O for any statement you feel is an opinion or interpretation of fact. Mark F for any statement you believe is a fact.*

If you are doing this activity as the member of a class or group, compare your answers with those of other class or group members. Be able to defend your answers. You may discover that others will come to different conclusions than you. Listening to the reasons others present for their answers may give you valuable insights in distinguishing between fact and opinion.

If you are reading this book alone, ask others if they agree with your answers. You too will find this interaction very valuable.

O = opinion
F = fact

1. The extinction of special privilege is an essential and basic program of the welfare state.

2. Individuals cannot be free if they are beset by fear and insecurity.

3. The Welfare State is not government *of* or *by* the people but *over* the people.

4. Universal equality of goods and services is the avowed aim of the Welfare State.

5. Capitalism has done more to eradicate poverty by the simple system of rewarding success and punishing failure, than any other system known to mankind.

6. The Welfare State kills political freedom and economic incentive.

7. The Welfare State necessitates a high degree of collective responsibility for children, the elderly, the disadvantaged, and the handicapped.

8. All Swedes and resident foreigners are covered upon registration by the national health insurance program.

9. In current language a Welfare State means a state where the care of dependent members is mostly performed by public agencies.

10. In Japan, people obviously have been able to successfully adapt to life conditions in a state with little public welfare.

11. The Welfare State, with "hired love" as one of the cornerstones, is virtually the most commercial state of all.

12. Full employment increases self-esteem, places persons in productive rather than dependent positions, and generates income rather than expenses for the national treasury.

13. Private charity is probably the only alternative to public welfare.

14. The poor will always be with us.

15. Like it or not, the Welfare State is a necessity in the contemporary world.

Bibliography

The following list of periodical articles deals with the subject matter of this chapter.

Nancy Amidei — "On Not Feeding the Hungry," *Commonweal*, April 10, 1981, p. 205.

Gregory Baum — "Moral People, Immoral Society," *The Witness*, October, 1980, p. 10.

James Breig — "The Poor Have a Right to Our Money," *U.S. Catholic*, August, 1982, p. 13.

Eric Brodin — "The End of the Swedish Welfare State," *New Guard*, Spring, 1981, p. 38.

George J. Church — "Are There Limits to Compassion?," *Time*, April 6, 1981, p. 12.

Jerry Flint — "How Sweden's Middle Road Becomes a Dead End," *Forbes*, April 27, 1981, p. 35.

Robert McNamara — "The Dimensions of Poverty," *Vital Speeches of the Day*, May 15, 1977, p. 450.

Michael Novak — "Rethinking Social Policy," *Worldview*, July/August, 1979, p. 40.

Phyllis Schlafly — "Moral Corruption of Welfare Statism," *Manchester Union Leader*, June 25, 1980.

George Seldes — "Repealing the General Welfare," *The Churchman*, January, 1982, p. 8.

Hans F. Sennholz — "Welfare States at War," *The Freeman*, April, 1981, p. 217.

Dean Snyder — "Thank God for the Train Stations," *The Christian Century*, November 28, 1979, p. 1177.

John R.W. Stott — "Who, Then, Are the Poor?," *Christianity Today*, May 8, 1981, p. 54.

Glen Tinder — "Defending the Welfare State," *The New Republic*, March 10, 1979, p. 21.

U.S. News & World Report — "When Welfare States Run into Hard Reality," May 27, 1980, p. 51.

Hans Zetterberg — "Maturing of the Swedish Welfare State," *Public Opinion*, October/November, 1979, p. 42.

Should the Welfare System Be Reformed?

"The financial ability of the states to provide fairly for the needs of the disadvantaged is much stronger now than it was 20 years ago."

Welfare Should Be Returned to the States

David A. Stockman

David A. Stockman is currently Director of the Office of Management and Budget for the Reagan administration. A former member of the U.S. House of Representatives from Southern Michigan, he was referred to in *Business Week* as "Reagan's economic powerhouse." The following viewpoint is taken from a statement presented by Mr. Stockman before the U.S. Senate Committee on Governmental Affairs, Senator William V. Roth, Jr., Chairman. In it, Mr. Stockman maintains that the recipients of public welfare would be better and more efficiently served by State funded assistance programs.

Consider the following questions while reading:
1. According to Mr. Stockman, what are the four fundamental attributes of "Fragmented Federalism?"
2. List some of the reasons why the author believes that the States can deal with their own welfare problems fairly and equitably.

Statement of David A. Stockman, Director of the Office of Management and Budget, before the Committee on Governmental Affairs, United States Senate, February 4, 1982.

The need to properly sort out Federal and State responsibilities has become increasingly clear to public officials, political scientists and intergovernmental bodies...

One of the best statements of the need for such major reordering of responsibilities I have found is in the remarks of the distinguished Chairman of this Committee. As Senator Roth pointed out over a year ago, "we no longer have the luxury of doing business as usual, for our Federal system is experiencing serious pressures which have been allowed to build for far too long." A few months later he explained: *"In the period since the great depression, and particularly in the last 20 years, we have seen massive changes in the nature of American Federalism. During this time we have moved from a Dual Federalism, where State and Federal government responsibilities were generally well defined and separate, through a stage of Cooperative Federalism, where some functions were shared, to our contemporary system which I chose to call Fragmented Federalism."*

The "Fragmented Federalism" identified by the Chairman has been distinguished by four fundamental attributes, each of which has crippled the ability of government at all levels to govern efficiently and responsively.

Four Reasons for Change

First, under the strain of its own growth, decisionmaking in Washington has broken down. As Senator Roth has pointed out, *"The Congress has expanded the role of the federal government to cover so many matters that the really important national priorities, for example defense, foreign policy and national economic issues, receive less attention than they deserve. Federal managers can hardly be expected to efficiently administer a federal establishment that does everything from patching pot holes to launching space craft."*

The tendency of the Federal Government to undertake ever-more projects — albeit poorly — undermines its ability to perform its essential responsibilities thoughtfully or well...

Second, the formerly clear Constitutional division of authority between Federal and State governments has been displaced by jurisdictional overlap and confusion of roles. The States, which once were sovereign entities with genuine governing authority over matters of the most vital interest to their citizens, have increasingly been used to implement *Federal* programs, with *Federal* money, under *Federal* control, to accomplish *Federal* objectives. To an alarming degree, the States have been reduced to mere administrative units of the Federal Government...

Third, without any clear principle for distinguishing Federal from State responsibilities and with all levels of government

43

responsible in some way for most programs, Federal, State and local government have increasingly engaged in competitive efforts to leave with the other the most expensive and politically unpopular responsibilities...

Fourth, today's system of "Fragmented Federalism" has eroded public confidence in government. The so-called "iron triangle" of executive branch bureaucracies, Congressional committee staffs, and interest groups has thrived on the expansion of federal authority through the grant-in-aid process. Lobbyists have flocked to Washington, where they now constitute the District's third largest industry, with an annual budget of $4 billion. Perhaps most poignantly, the once-sovereign States now find themselves merely one leg of that "iron triangle," competing with the other lobbyists for Federal attention...

The Profound Changes in the States

The redirection of national authority and power...would have been unthinkable had not the States, individually and collectively, established a remarkable record for fair, representative, efficient, and responsive government. As the Advisory Commission on Intergovernmental Relations has concluded, *"A largely unnoticed revolution has occured in state government. The states have been transformed to a remarkable degree. The decades of the 1960s and 1970s witnessed changes in state government unparalleled since the post-Reconstruction period a century ago, generally in the direction advocated by reformers for 50 years."*

Increased State Aid

To those who have said you can't trust certain states to provide for their poor, the fact is that in the last 10 or 15 years there has been a tremendous change in this country. States, particularly in the South, that have had a history of low benefit levels have been increasing their benefits to the poor.

Robert B. Carleson, *Human Events*, July 30, 1977.

The evidence of increasing State ability to assume responsibilities under the Federalism initiative is impressive and undeniable. Twenty years ago, all but five State legislatures were badly malaportioned. Now, every State has apportioned its legislature on the basis of one person, one vote. During the same period, the participation of racial and ethnic minorities in the electoral process has dramatically increased. Between 1960 and 1980, black voter registration in the 11 Southern states rose from 29.1% of the voting age population to 59.8%. Moreover, while a quarter of a century ago many states were

WHERE THE 'NEW FEDERALISM' BUCK STOPS

ruled by one political party, without effective opposition; today one-party states are a phenomenon of the past. Since 1968, no single party has held a monopoly on Senatorial and gubernatorial positions in any State.

Concern has been expressed about the willingness and ability of the states to take care of disadvantaged Americans. On this point, we should recognize that there are cliches and there are realities, and one reality is that the same electorate which chooses Senators and Congressmen also elects governors, mayors, and legislators. There is no reason to believe that...the American people have two minds, two hearts, and two agendas regarding the responsibility of government to meet genuine social needs. Every indication is that citizen participation at the State and local level on behalf of such causes as the environment, ethnic and racial minorities, the disadvantaged, tax reform, the handicapped, and electoral reform has grown significantly in vigor and sophistication since the mid-60s.

The financial ability of the States to provide fairly for the needs of the disadvantaged is also much stronger now than it was 20 years ago. State revenue sources have become significantly more diversified and resilient. Thirty-six states now have a corporate and personal income tax, as well as a general sales tax, compared to only 19 in 1960. Past regional differences in wealth have narrowed dramatically. As an example, every State in the Southeast has experienced growth in per capita income since 1970 at a rate exceeding the national average...

The Dilemma, The Solution

The continuing tie to Federal financing has demanded, in the name of program and fiscal accountability, that grantees be buried under a blizzard of cumbersome and often conflicting requirements that, taken together, greatly reduce the capacity of our partners in the Federal system to adequately meet the needs of their citizens.

The clear answer to this dilemma is to break the tie that binds other units of government to Federal tax sources, and to provide a means whereby States and other units of government are able to meet pressing local needs out of locally-generated revenues, under locally generated standards of accountability.

David A. Stockman

*"Dismantling of the federal government's
constitutional responsibilities to promote the
general welfare amounts to a resurrection of
the discredited concept of states' rights."*

Welfare Should Not Be Returned to the States

Vernon E. Jordan, Jr.

President of the National Urban League, Vernon E. Jordan, Jr. is one of the leading and most influential black civil rights leaders in the United States today. The following viewpoint is taken from a speech he delivered to the Council on Social Work Education annual program meeting in Louisville, Kentucky. In it, Mr. Jordan explains why he believes that federal welfare programs should not be returned to the states. Although some states may administer welfare fairly and wisely, the historical record, he claims, clearly demonstrates that many would abuse the rights of the poor.

Consider the following questions while reading:
1. What lessons does Mr. Jordan say black people can teach about states' rights?
2. What are the reasons the author gives for opposing a return of welfare programs to state control?
3. What examples does Mr. Jordan give to support retention of federal control of welfare programs and what is one conservative solution to the welfare problem he would support?

Vernon E. Jordan, Jr., "The Surrender of Federal Programs to the States," *Vital Speeches of the Day*, May 1, 1981. Reprinted by permission of *Vital Speeches*.

The social work profession today is challenged as perhaps never before. The enlightened, compassionate ideals of ending poverty, discrimination and inequality are under siege. They are no longer in fashion. Years of recession and inflation have created a meaner America, an America unwilling to build a better society for all...

"The Grand Design"

Widespread black and white deprivation must be the context in which the social work profession responds to the Administration's radical budget proposals. Those proposals are the subject of a national debate in which the voices of the poor are muted and the voices of a new negativism are loud...

This budget is just the first skirmish of a war to reverse totally the direction of national domestic policies. The outlines of that war were described in a *Wall Street Journal* editorial, entitled "The Grand Design," which said: *"...the Administration means to go much further. The first step is to channel the cuts into block grants. The second is to return whole functions to the states."*

We face then, a new policy of shifting federal dollars, federal responsibilities, and federal powers, to the fifty states. The current budget packages over eighty separate programs in health and education into block grants to the states to be administered with a minimum of federal control. And the cap on Medicaid implies that a major entitlement program will become a ward of the states.

This "Grand Design" must be resisted by advocates of the poor, including social workers. For this dismantling of the federal government's constitutional responsibilities to promote the general welfare amounts to a resurrection of the discredited concept of states' rights.

Black people could teach the nation a bit about states' rights. We know states' rights meant separate drinking fountains, separate schools, separate and unequal lives. We know that today, state administration of federal programs such as welfare, Medicaid, and others is inefficient and often discriminatory. We know that state and local administration is a large part of the reason why eligibility rules are ignored to the extent that nearly half of black welfare families are excluded from Medicaid.

So while we must oppose budget cuts in programs that do work, we must prepare for the even tougher battle against block grants and the surrender of federal programs to the states.

Look At the Record

Some states can be relied upon to institute and administer programs for the benefit of the disadvantaged. But the histori-

"But that's where we just came from!"

Reprinted by permission of the *Daily World*.

cal record, and the record of the current urban block grant programs, clearly demonstrates that many would abuse the rights of the poor.

Some state and local authorities make a persuasive argument for putting control of programs closer to the people they serve. But local authorities are far more vulnerable to local power structures and voting blocs that would end those programs.

Many states would treat the poor equitably. But rights embedded by law in federal entitlement programs would go by the boards. Twenty years of federal court decisions protecting the basic civil and human rights of program recipients would be wiped out by changing the ground rules of those programs.

The search for local solutions to social problems must be encouraged. But localizing solutions to national problems tends to compound those problems.

Federal social programs should meet clear criteria: they should be national in scope, accountable, efficient, and equitable. The block grant system violates every one of those criteria.

It would make about as much sense to turn national defense into a block grant program and rely on state National Guards for our security. Absurd, isn't it? Yet that is what we propose to do with programs essential for our domestic national security and well-being.

Those of us who have a vision of an open, pluralistic, integrated society, have the duty to resist an increase in the misery inflicted on poor people and increase the ranks of America's deprived. We must question not only specific budget cuts, but the Grand Design of pushing the poor deeper into the pit of poverty.

The Big Lie

We must educate the American public to the need for key social programs and explode the Big Lie that those programs don't work.

In fact, they do work. Food Stamps have just about wiped out hunger in America. Studies of Head Start programs prove that participating children do better in school than others. Job Corps graduates get better jobs than those without training in that program. Other programs have effectively helped millions of people to get productive jobs, decent housing, health care and education. They are investments in America's productivity and strength.

And those are not, as the Big Lie has it, minority programs. The majority of welfare recipients are white. Four out of five people getting Medicaid and special programs for the aged are white. White people are in the majority in Section 8 housing subsidy programs, in CETA jobs, and in most other programs bearing the "black" label. Defending the needs of the minority poor means also defending the forgotten white poor.

The Big Lie blames social programs for inflation and economic stagnation. But those social programs came into being — and exist today — to protect those most victimized by our economy's failures. Their cost is but a fraction of non-productive military expenditures — the MX missile system would eat up far more tax dollars than the Food Stamp Program.

Most of the federal budget programs stigmatized as examples of swollen spending on the poor are not programs for the poor at all, but benefit middle class Americans. Those programs targeted only to the poor hardly make a dent in the economy, especially when contrasted with the twenty-five percent of the budget set aside for the military, a figure that will go to 33 percent in four years...

Some Creative Alternatives

There are creative alternatives to social programs that need reforming. The welfare system, for example, is shot through with gross inequities. Not one single state provides benefit levels that, even with food stamps added, bring families up to the inadequate poverty line. It is a system of administrative abuses, red tape, and irrationality. It is a prescription for perpetuating poverty.

Turning welfare over to the states would just compound those evils. That is demonstrated by current state administration. A truly conservative solution to the welfare problem would be one that puts cash directly into the hands of the poor, reduces the red tape and bureaucracy that has such arbitrary power over people, and gives to the poor the same freedom of choice and the same responsibilities enjoyed by others.

So a conservative solution to welfare points to the plan the National Urban League has advanced — an income maintenance system based on the credit income tax. Our plan would ensure that all people have minimum income protection and maximum freedom. It is a realistic alternative to the monster system that serves both the nation and poor people badly.

Our task is to defend the interests of the poor, and to present alternatives to a forgetting nation. More is at stake than cutting budgets or experimenting with radical economic theories. What is at stake in America's treatment of its poor people and its minorities is nothing less than the historic vision of an America devoted to equality and to justice.

At stake is Lincoln's definition of America's purpose as being *"to lift artificial weights from all shoulders; to clear the path of laudable pursuits for all; to afford all an unfettered start and a fair chance in life."*

"Public welfare destroys the personal relationship and interaction which can be achieved through private, local charity."

Charities Should Care for the Poor

Kenneth L. Gentry, Jr.

Kenneth L. Gentry, Jr. is currently a minister at the Reedy River Presbyterian Church, Greenville, South Carolina. A graduate of Tennessee Temple University (BA) and Reformed Theological Seminary (Master of Divinity), Reverend Gentry is a contributing author and editor for numerous religious and secular publications. In the following viewpoint, he outlines 17 reasons why he believes that charity originating in the private sector should replace public welfare.

Consider the following questions while reading:
1. Why does Rev. Gentry believe public welfare destroys genuine charity?
2. Why does the author accuse public welfare of creating a false sense of security and a false sense of equality?
3. What are the three functions he believes government could properly perform to care for the needy?

Kenneth L. Gentry, Jr., "The Problems with Public Welfare," *The Freeman*, November, 1979.

Americans have long been known to be a charitable people. Unfortunately, government intervention could be changing that. The government has entered and gained monopolistic ascendancy in this field as in so many others. Being charitable makes it a bit difficult for us to speak out against public welfarism, lest we appear to be unconcerned for the needs of the poor. However, there are numerous compelling reasons why we can legitimately decry public welfarism and still maintain — even *emphasize* — our concern for the less fortunate in our society.

Welfare Destroys Relationships, Charity

1. Public welfare destroys the personal relationship and interaction which can be achieved through private, local charity. Big government is faceless and cannot express truly empathetic concern for the needy. The human element so essential to aid the poor is sacrificed to computerization.

2. It actually destroys a true sense of genuine charity among the general populace. Charity today is coercively maintained. How many times have you heard complaints about excessive taxation? And what accounts for a very large percentage of our national debt? I used to work in a grocery store and constantly overheard grumbling from the shoppers who were having to pinch their pennies when they observed a heavily loaded shopping cart of choice items being paid for with food stamps. Not only are ill feelings fostered but also there is provided an excuse to shift responsibility when private charities appeal for funds: "The government has the resources. They will handle the situation."

3. It destroys, through excessive taxation, the capacity of private citizens and organizations to help. Personal income is eroded through redistributive tax schemes, thus leaving fewer funds for personal charity...

4. It undermines personal responsibility and incentive in the poor to help themselves. Welfare funds are addictive. Withdrawal is hard.

5. It promotes a false sense of security among the needy. "The government will always be there to take care of me." "My Social Security will always be available to help me financially." According to the Federal Statement of Liabilities issued by the Treasury Department, the Social Security program has about $4 *trillion* in *unfunded* obligations! That's security?

6. It promotes a false sense of equality among minorities. They can either be led to believe they are getting their "fair share" or that they are receiving "remuneration" for past offenses against them. Dependency does *not* promote equality.

Public Welfare is Inefficient

7. It is less efficient than private charity. Private, local charity

53

is true charity: it is voluntary and it is not subject to the bureaucratic filtering process. I have never heard the government or any of its programs praised for efficiency — except by the government and those who head the programs!

8. It promotes conflict among groups clamoring to get their hands on the handouts...

9. It can and often does encourage immorality. The government does not have the same degree of religious and moral sensitivity that can characterize private charities. Illegitimate children are one way to gain additional welfare funds. Or if you decide against illegitimacy, in most cases you can get a "free" abortion. Urban renewal programs have long been derided as consistently producing drug culture, crime infestation areas, and family disruption.

Kenneth L. Gentry, Jr.

10. It is more open to fraud and criminal abuse than smaller, more easily contained, private charity programs. Newspapers are filled with reports of welfare abuse by criminal elements. This serves as an additional "tax" on the truly needy themselves: scarce resources are filtered away from their target.

11. It destroys the incentive to produce among the heavily taxed middle class. Success seems to be subject to undue fines (increased taxation).

12. It represents a large percentage of the federal debt that is monetized in the process of inflation. Price inflation erodes the wealth of the nation and will eventually break the back of the economy...

13. It is ironic that the expansionistic monetary policies of the government which are partly necessitated by welfare programs are not only hurting the general well-being of the nation at large but are especially hurtful to those on fixed incomes: the welfare recipients for whom we inflate in order to aid! The government is sadistic: it whips hardest the very people it supposedly wants to help.

14. It coerces medical personnel to give out "free" services... This not only raises prices for the non-welfare populace, but when medical programs are further expanded they cause medical shortages...

Welfare Promotes Power of State

15. It increases statist power. That which controls your property and wealth controls *you*. A bigger government is more unmanageable, more susceptible to totalitarianism and tyranny. Thus, it aids and abets the erosion of liberty. Higher taxes cut down on what we are able to do, increased regulations (concocted by a powerful state) limit what we are allowed to do.

What Private Help Offers

We all need what only private philanthropy can offer. We need its compassion. We need its understanding of human frailty. We need its availability in times of stress, and of danger, and of deprivation. We need its concern for the poor, the weak, the uncertain, the frightened.

James F. Bere, *USA Today*, March, 1982.

---

16. It unmasks "blind" justice. It coercively redistributes the wealth from some in order to favor others — all in the name of social "justice"! Discriminating justice is mandatory injustice.

17. It encourages an increased ignorance in one of the most important areas of life in our population: economics. "Free" programs imply that wealth is "just there," profits are evil, shortages are contrived, lunches can be free. Our population already suffers a woeful ignorance of economic theory, without interventionist politics setting a bad example.

Yet despite these problems and others that could easily be multiplied, there are certain functions which government could properly perform to care for the needy.

Proper Functions of Government

First, the central feature of the government is power. The purpose of this power is to insure the law and order necessary for economic stability and growth. As F. A. Hayek has written in *The Constitution of Liberty*: "There is probably no single factor which has contributed more to the prosperity of the West than the relative certainty of the law which has prevailed here." A wealthier people can better support the needy. The government can promote wealth through law and order.

Second, the government could abandon its redistributive schemes, reduce the burden of direct taxes and inflation, and leave to productive individuals the means and the incentive to help their less fortunate neighbors. Charitable giving is much more efficient than coercive redistribution.

Third, the state can use its judicial power to prosecute criminal and fraudulent abuses of charity.

The state *does* have a concern for the welfare of its population. The only legitimate way and the best way to care for the poor is through encouraging charity in the private sector by the three-fold method outlined above.

"Private charity, alone, cannot realistically, effectively or systematically remedy (welfare) problems. Government can and must."

Welfare Is the Government's Responsibility

Michael Meyers

Michael Meyers is currently Assistant Director for the National Association for the Advancement of Colored People (NAACP). A graduate of Antioch College and Rutgers University School of Law, he has written numerous articles for the *New York Times, Los Angeles Times, Washington Post, Change* magazine and others. Mr. Meyers previously served as Principle Assistant to Dr. Kenneth B. Clark, President of the Metropolitan Applied Research Center, Inc., New York. In the following viewpoint, he outlines certain current misconceptions regarding welfare and explains why it is morally imperative that government maintain a compassionate, visible and more active role in assisting those leading marginal lives.

Consider the following questions while reading:

1. According to the author, what public assistance programs are included under the "welfare umbrella?"
2. According to Mr. Meyers, how does the media contribute to public misconceptions on welfare?

The following viewpoint was written specifically for this book. The editor wishes to express his deep appreciation to Mr. Meyers and the NAACP.

Americans can communicate across space instantaneously but they have not successfully communicated the facts about welfare across the distances of race and class. So, the average citizen doesn't yet know that most people on Welfare are white, not black; that rich people also are subsidized by government; or that blacks are disproportionately poor because of the patterns of racial discrimination throughout American life.

These facts are important to debunking the myths about Welfare. But even those individuals personally friendly toward the idea of government assistance to the needy are mesmerized by its skyrocketing costs, the concommitant burden on the taxpayer, and the sensational reports of the able-bodied getting a "free-ride" on the welfare rolls. This frustration has been unabashedly exploited by a succession of politicians who, as recently as the 1980 elections, blamed welfare and "welfare cheats" for high taxation, and for the erosion of the work ethic...

Welfare Concerns All

However, some people see that *Welfare* is broader than any program for families with dependent children; it is, also, social security; unemployment insurance; medicaid and medicare; aid to cities and agricultural areas; support for educational institutions and students; funding for health care facilities and patients; and longstanding support systems for the infrastructure that creates jobs for white and blue-collar workers. Welfare is the tax breaks given to builders of luxury housing as well as the subsidies provided for low-income projects. It is tax loopholes for the rich and earned income credits for the poor.

Welfare is everybody's concern and every government's responsibility. This is becoming clearer now that the newspapers tell the story of the soup-kitchens, the plight of college students who can no longer afford to stay in school, the longer waits for commuter buses and trains, and, because of reduced government subsidies, the rise in transit fares...

The media has not always been responsible, however, in reporting the facts about Welfare in America. Rare are the exceptional human-interest documentaries such as Bill Moyers' on CBS, and the spectacular revelations of a David Stockman, in *Atlantic Monthly*, about the government's *trojan horse* strategy to enrich the wealthiest at the expense of the poor. More often the media emphasizes the welfare fraud arrests, and popularize stereotypes about "welfare types." For example, journalist Ken Auletta recently published a series of articles (adapted from his book, *The Underclass*) on the Welfare Poor. In one he interviews an unwed "welfare mother" who, we are told, has some 28 children and is illustrative of "the passive poor."

"Nothing like helping the needy. Put it here.

How many people will draw the wrong inferences from such a bizarre and *atypical* welfare case! How many readers will tap into the myth that there really is such a type as "the welfare mother?" Many will. And they will picture her as black because many Americans believe in stereotypes and ignore facts. They believe that "the welfare problem" is the black, fat, lazy woman with dozens of illegitimate children. With that prejudice goes the saying, "they don't want to work. But they have plenty of time to make babies." These lines are matched with horrendous stories of black children running wild in the streets, and babies having babies in order to keep the welfare check coming...

"A Moral Imperative"

The existence of ghettoes, the conditions which unequal treatment and overt racial discrimination generate, contradict any suggestion that the time has come to end an affirmative role for government in eradicating poverty, increasing the supply of affordable and decent housing, and improving the health and quality of life for all Americans. Private charity, alone, cannot realistically, effectively or systematically remedy such problems. Government can and must.

We had better start thinking more clearly and compassionately about Welfare if we are to avoid a cataclysmic collision between the have-nots and those who control the political and economic power in our society. This is no idle threat; it is a moral imperative. We cannot hope for a stable and democratic society if government doesn't act to mitigate the hurt and tragedies that beset individuals and families in poverty, by no fault of their own. This is especially urgent since there has been no reticence on the part of government, at all levels, to protect the rights, and sustain the privileges, of the wealthiest individuals and families in America.

> *"Today's welfare system, despite its
> shortcomings, is a relatively good one."*

Welfare Reform Is Not Necessary

William P. Albrecht

William P. Albrecht is Associate Professor of Economics at the University of Iowa. The following viewpoint is an excerpt from a speech on welfare reform which he delivered at the Second Middlebury College Conference on Economic Issues in Iowa City, Iowa. In it, he outlines what he believes should be the key features of an efficient welfare system and then concludes that the existing system in the U.S. is "reasonably satisfactory."

Consider the following questions while reading:
1. What eight characteristics does the author say are essential for a good welfare system?
2. What are the two basic reasons which Professor Albrecht says prevent welfare reform?

William P. Albrecht, "Welfare Reform — An Idea Whose Time Has Come and Gone," *Vital Speeches of the Day*, October 15, 1980. Reprinted by permission of *Vital Speeches.*

The United States' multibillion dollar welfare system is hardly a system at all. It is a melange of uncoordinated programs which have been created by a variety of legislative bodies and which are administered by a variety of federal, state and local agencies. As a result, welfare benefits vary widely from person to person and from state to state.

The many apparent shortcomings of our welfare system have, over the past decade, led to persistent demands for welfare reform. These demands continue to be heard from presidents, governors, legislators, taxpayers, welfare recipients and participants in conferences on welfare reform. Such demands, however, are both futile and unwarranted. They are unwarranted; because today's welfare system, despite its shortcomings, is a relatively good one. These demands are futile, because welfare reform is dead politically.

The Politics of Welfare Reform

The reason for asserting that welfare reform is dead is a simple one: *welfare reform will not be enacted by Congress; it is politically impossible...*

The experience with President Nixon's welfare reform proposals in 1970 and President Carter's proposals in 1978 provide empirical support for this political judgment. As an example, consider the fate of Carter's attempt to create 1.4 million public service jobs. Under Carter's proposal many people would be classified as "expected to work." Since experience suggested that there would not be private sector jobs available for all those expected to work, a jobs program was an important element in the President's approach to welfare reform. Despite widespread agreement that a good welfare system would encourage people to work, not everyone agreed that a jobs program was desirable. Many were opposed to additional federal spending. Others, while not opposed to expansion of the government sector in general, wondered about the effectiveness of such a massive jobs program. Supporting the idea of a jobs program were many of those belonging to the natural constituency for welfare reform. Their support was critical to enactment of a jobs program, but they could not agree with others or the President over the details of the program. Some of them, such as the National Association of Social Workers (NASW) criticized the plan for not providing enough jobs...

The moral of this little episode is clear. There will be no jobs program which provides adequate job opportunities for unskilled, low income people who cannot obtain employment in the private sector. If there is a jobs program, most of the jobs will pay more than the minimum wage, thereby making the program so expensive that there will be fewer jobs created than are needed. Additionally, the high wage rate will make the jobs attractive to relatively skilled workers, and the low skill individuals for whom the program was proposed will not get the jobs...

A Vested Interest in Welfare

Too many people have vested interests in existing welfare programs to permit reform to occur. The only way in which change can occur is to placate the relevant interest groups by giving each one something it wants. Accordingly, the only significant changes in the welfare system which are likely to occur are incremental increases in benefit levels and incremental increases in the number of people on the welfare rolls. Certainly this is exactly what has happened to all previous attempts at welfare reform, and there is little reason to believe things will change. In fact, there is less and less reason to expect change, because there are more and more people with a stake in the existing system. As the process of incrementally increasing the welfare budget continues, movement toward a significantly different system becomes increasingly unlikely...

The impossibility of welfare reform does not mean that we are doomed to live with a terrible system. On the contrary, the existing system has a number of the features that many believe should be found in a good welfare system. Furthermore, it is not at all clear that any existing proposals for reform (were they miraculously enacted) would unambiguously improve the system...

There appears to be general agreement that a good welfare system will have the following characteristics: 1) adequate benefits, 2) vertical equity, 3) horizontal equity, 4) target efficiency, 5) administrative efficiency, 6) adequate work incentives, 7) adequate work opportunities, and 8) responsiveness to individual needs. Agreeing on the desirability of these characteristics, however, still leaves considerable room for disagreement. One source of disagreement is over the specifics of each of these features. As these terms are defined or discussed below, some of the problems involved in determining specific program characteristics become apparent.

Characteristics of Good Welfare System

1. *Adequate benefits.* The chief purpose of any welfare program is to provide some people with a better standard of living. But how much better? What is adequate? Is it poverty line income? Sixty-five percent of poverty line income? One hundred fifty percent? And who should receive these adequate benefits? All people with low incomes? Only those "unable to work" or "not expected to work"?

2. *Vertical equity.* Families with higher pre-transfer incomes should have higher post-transfer incomes, but how much higher? By the full differences in the pre-transfer incomes? Or by some percentage? What percentage?

3. *Horizontal equity.* Families in similar circumstances should receive similar benefits. But what factors determine similar circumstances? How similar are the circumstances of a low income family with two adults present to those of a family of the same size with only one adult present? How similar is a family with educated, skilled adults to a family with uneducated, unskilled adults?

4. *Target efficiency.* This means that benefits should be concentrated on those most in need. It means the most possible assistance to the needy for each dollar of benefits delivered. But what is the best way to give assistance? Are cash payments or in-kind payments more efficient?

5. *Adequate work incentives.* To most economists, this means a low income guarantee and a low marginal tax rate (benefit reduction rate). Benefits must be reduced by less than one dollar for each dollar of earned income. But how much? Does a marginal tax rate of 30 percent provide adequate incentives? Does 40 percent?

6. *Adequate work opportunities.* A desire to work is not enough; jobs must be available. This means high aggregate demand is a necessary condition for a successful welfare program. But is it a sufficient condition? Or should government help create specific jobs for welfare recipients? Can this be done through private employers? Or are public sector jobs also required? If so, at what wage rates?

7. *Administrative efficiency.* The welfare system should deliver a given level of benefits at the lowest possible cost. This is a fairly straightforward proposition, but it is impossible to determine whether this goal has been achieved. Some people will always argue that there are too many bureaucrats employed by the system, but others will argue for hiring more people in order to reduce fraud or to provide more individual attention for people with special needs.

8. *Responsiveness to individual needs.* A good welfare system must be more than a computerized operation run from a central location. Welfare recipients have financial and other emergencies which require special or immediate assistance. Needs may vary regionally or seasonally. The critical question is how many resources should be devoted to this feature of the welfare system.

The preceding discussion of the specifics of a welfare system may seem to belabor the obvious, but it does raise important issues which are often overlooked by critics of the existing system. Furthermore, the difficulty of giving specific content to each of the eight items is increased by the fact that many of the eight characteristics, however specified, are incompatible with one another...

Reform is Not Possible

This paper has set forth two basic reasons for arguing that welfare reform's time has come and gone. The first is that reform or a significant change in the structure of this system is no longer (if it ever was) politically possible. Too many people have a stake in the existing system to permit changes that are significant enough to be labeled reform. Those with a stake in the existing system include more than welfare recipients and those responsible for administering the systems. For example, organized labor strongly opposed two proposals which many people consider essential to welfare reform — low wage public sector jobs and lowering the minimum wage.

The second reason for suggesting that we forget about welfare reform is that the existing system is reasonably satisfactory (and will be more satisfactory with the addition of SWRA, Social Welfare Reform Amendments of 1979). Certainly, the strong opposition to reform suggests that it is reasonably satisfactory to many people, but the argument is stronger than that. The argument is not just that reform will reduce the incomes of a number of people and should, therefore, be avoided. The basic argument is that the existing system represents a relatively satisfactory mixture of the features which we would like to see in a welfare system. Furthermore, movement toward a more unified federal system will not necessarily improve the system. For every benefit generated by reforms there will be a cost. On balance it is not entirely obvious that the net benefits would be positive.

"The welfare state...promotes the very kind of unemployment, family breakdown and economic stagnation that it is supposed to cure."

Welfare Reform Is Necessary

George Gilder

George Gilder is currently program director of the International Center for Economic Policy Studies in New York. His best-selling book, *Wealth and Poverty*, is said to have greatly influenced present day supporters of "supply side" economics. A contributor to *The Wall Street Journal* and many other publications, Mr. Gilder has also written *Sexual Suicide* and *Visible Man*. In the following viewpoint, he claims that state welfarism actually promotes many of the social and economic ills which it is supposed to cure.

Consider the following questions while reading:

1. Why does Mr. Gilder believe that "looking out for No. 1" is dangerous to a capitalist society?
2. Why does the author contend that welfare promotes the very problems it was meant to cure?
3. According to Mr. Gilder, what is the best welfare system?

George Gilder, "Welfare State Promotes What It Is Supposed to Cure," April 6, 1981. Reprinted from *U.S. News & World Report*, Copyright 1981, U.S. News & World Report, Inc.

Many of our problems as a society come from an increasingly secular pursuit of self-interest, often defined as pleasure. This pursuit leads to ever greater demands for comfort and security. It leads us — as by an invisible hand — to an ever growing welfare state and, hence, to economic stagnation. Those who stress "looking out for No. 1" virtually give up on the system; they end up with doomsday visions that impair the faith in the future that is crucial to capitalist growth.

The bureaucrats seek a fail-safe society in which the creative human activity that produces economic growth is increasingly retarded. If we continue down that road, we will no longer have the riches of growth that are the American miracle.

"Family Disintegration" — Stigma of the Inner City

The welfare state in the United States and in other parts of the world promotes the very kind of unemployment, family breakdown and economic stagnation that it is supposed to cure.

This is demonstrated by what has happened since the Great Society programs came into being in the mid-60's. Before that, blacks were making steady and impressive progress. Since then, there has been progress only among middle-class blacks.

In the various inner cities, where these programs focus their attention, virtually all families are now female headed. The indices of family breakdown and illegitimacy have more than doubled since 1965. It isn't the amount of money the families receive that is a problem — there's no way anyone can say that benefits worth $15,000 a year are impossible to live on — the problem is family disintegration.

Female-headed families cannot escape poverty. If their welfare payments increase, their problems grow more serious because it becomes more difficult for them to envision a society in which people's rewards are connected with their work. Boys, in particular, brought up in female-headed families have great trouble adjusting to a disciplined, productive life. They have no male role models and pursue their masculinity on the street with gangs.

Poverty: "More a Matter of Prospects than Income"

The only source of income that grows as the family grows is welfare. That means any large family has a great propensity to go on welfare. If you give all the rewards in poor communities to women with kids, you end up with a lot of women with kids.

These large families need a father more than any other kind of family. But if you provide the money to the mother in proportion to the number of children she has, the father is likely to leave. His departure has nothing to do with state laws that require fathers not to be on the premises; his leaving is a function of the loss of the provider role, which is crucial to men. Any government program that renders the man optional will lead to his departure. He no longer feels affirmed in his role in the family.

The contention of some poverty statisticians that we've virtually abolished poverty in America is preposterous. Poverty is worse than before. You can be completely impoverished, even with a $20,000-a-year income, if you are incapable of coping or alcoholic or addicted.

Real poverty is more a matter of prospects than of income. A family with no hope and with children verging on delinquency will seem impoverished even if their income is fairly high. The idea that poverty is a matter of objective income standards is nonsense.

Reprinted with permission of *The Union Leader*, Manchester, NH. Copyright 1982.

"The Most Immoral Aspect of American Liberalism"

One of the more irritating ideas is that anybody who criticizes the welfare system wants people out on the streets. It is the welfare system that breaks down families and drives fathers into the streets.

The fact is that the chief enemies of a rational welfare system are people who refuse to reduce the current level of benefits. They continually cut back on the fringes of the system in the belief that there are some deserving poor who should receive very great benefits — twice as great as the income from a job at the minimum wage — while there are all these undeserving poor out there whom the government can identify and kick off the rolls.

This always means that the government behaves in a very brutal way while at the same time creating huge incentives for the poor to wildly distort their lives in order to qualify for benefits that are far greater than any job could yield them. This is not compassionate; it's the most immoral aspect of American liberalism. We have destroyed the black family in America's slums.

The best welfare system gives low benefits and makes them available to people in emergencies who need it...

In the final analysis, redistributing income is a very corrupting and destructive process. It hurts both the people who are taxed and those who receive it. It should be pursued as cautiously as possible.

Recognizing Stereotypes

A stereotype is an oversimplified or exaggerated description of people or things. Stereotyping can be favorable. However, most stereotyping tends to be highly uncomplimentary and, at times, degrading.

Stereotyping grows out of our prejudices. When we stereotype someone, we are prejudging him or her. Consider the following example: Mr. X is convinced that all Mexicans are lazy, sloppy and careless people. The Diaz family, a family of Mexicans, happen to be his next-door neighbors. One evening, upon returning home from work, Mr. X notices that the garbage pails in the Diaz driveway are overturned and that the rubbish is scattered throughout the driveway. He immediately says to himself: "Isn't that just like those lazy, sloppy and careless Mexicans?" The possibility that a group of neighborhood vandals or a pack of stray dogs may be responsible for the mess never enters his mind. Why not? Simply because he has prejudged all Mexicans and will keep his stereotype consistent with his prejudice. The famous (or infamous) Archie Bunker of television fame is a classic example of our Mr. X.

Most of the following statements are taken from the viewpoints in this chapter. The rest are taken from other sources. Consider each statement carefully. *Mark S for any statement that is an example of stereotyping. Mark N for any statement that is not an example of stereotyping. Mark U if you are undecided about any statement.*

If you are doing this activity as the member of a class or group, compare your answers with those of other class or group members. Be able to defend your answers. You may discover that others will come to different conclusions than you. Listening to the reasons others present for their answers may give you valuable insights in recognizing stereotypes.

If you are reading this book alone, ask others if they agree with your answers. You too will find this interaction very valuable.

> S = *stereotype*
> N = *not a stereotype*
> U = *undecided*

1. Over the past twenty years, the participation of racial and ethnic minorities in the electoral process has dramatically increased.

2. Black people could teach the nation a bit about states' rights. We know states' rights meant separate drinking fountains, separate schools, separate and unequal lives.

3. Four out of five people getting Medicaid and special programs for the aged are white.

4. Big government is faceless and cannot express truly empathetic concern for the needy.

5. Public welfare is more open to fraud and criminal abuse than smaller, more easily contained, private charity programs.

6. The United States' multibillion dollar welfare system is hardly a system at all. It is a mixture of uncoordinated programs.

7. The existing welfare system in the United States has a number of the features that many believe should be found in a good welfare system.

8. The Welfare State in the United States and in other parts of the world promotes the very kind of unemployment, family breakdown and economic stagnation that it is supposed to cure.

9. The contention of some poverty statisticians that we've virtually abolished poverty in America is preposterous.

10. The fact is that the chief enemies of a rational welfare system are people who refuse to reduce the current level of benefits.

11. Minority groups tend to abuse their welfare privileges more often than others.

12. People will not want to work if they can collect welfare.

13. Only private charity can show concern for the poor, the weak, the uncertain, the frightened. Public agencies cannot.

14. People living in countries where there is no welfare system tend to be more industrious.

15. All conservatives oppose the Welfare State; all liberals support it.

Bibliography

The following list of periodical articles deals with the subject matter of this chapter.

Samuel H. Beer — "The Idea of the Nation," *The New Republic*, July 19 & 26, 1982, p. 23.

A. Cherlin — "Welfare Reform, Take Five," *New Republic*, June 30, 1979, p. 10.

Robert Cizik — "The Challenge of Less Government," *Vital Speeches of the Day*, June 15, 1982, p. 523.

Congressional Digest — "The Welfare Reform Amendments Act," January, 1980.

Winston Davis — "The Gospel According to Gilder," *Christianity and Crisis*, February 1, 1982, p. 11.

Pierre S. du Point — "The New Federalism," *Vital Speeches of the Day*, June 15, 1982, p. 523.

Dorothy M. Forney — "United Welfare Fraud Council Battling To Stop the Ripoff of Billions in Tax Dollars," *Conservative Digest*, August, 1981, p. 30.

Meg Greenfield — "The Numbers Racket," *Newsweek*, October 5, 1981, p. 94.

"The War about Poverty," *Newsweek*, May 3, 1982, p. 92.

Nick Kotz — "The War on the Poor," *The New Republic*, March 24, 1982, p. 18.

National Review — "George Gilder's Wealth and Poverty: A Symposium," April 17, 1981, p. 414.

Newsweek — "How the Poor Will Be Hurt," March 23, 1981, p. 23.

A. Poinsett — "Who Gets Welfare?," *Ebony*, January, 1982, p. 26.

Thomas J. Reese — "Who Is Poor?," *America*, May 1, 1982, p. 333.

Marvin Stone — "The Welfare Monstrosity," *U.S. News & World Report*, February 1, 1982, p. 72.

Robert Joe Stout — "I'm Not Your Typical Welfare Case...," *Commonweal*, June 5, 1981, p. 333.

Robert Joe Stout — "I'm Not Your Typical Welfare Case...," *Commonweal*, June 5, 1981, p. 333.

Edmund C. Szoka — "The Church's Concern for Social and Economic Well-Being," *Vital Speeches of the Day*, March 1, 1982, p. 292.

What is the Role
of Social Security?

"Through the years since social security was enacted there have been many changes to improve the protection it gives to workers and their families."

Social Security Benefits Everyone

Department of Health, Education and Welfare

The social security program in the United States was enacted in 1935. It was one of the many public welfare programs legislated by Congress during the "New Deal" of Franklin D. Roosevelt. Today, social security falls under the umbrella of the Department of Health, Education and Welfare (HEW), a cabinet level department. The following viewpoint is taken from the pamphlet *Your Social Security* published by HEW. In it, many of the benefits available to eligible social security recipients are outlined.

Consider the following questions while reading:

1. According to HEW, why does nearly every family in the U.S. have a stake in social security?
2. How does HEW explain the way social security works to provide retirement benefits? To provide medical insurance benefits?
3. According to HEW, how is social security financed?

Your Social Security, HEW Publication No. (SSA) 78-10035, August, 1978. U.S. Department of Health, Education and Welfare.

Today, social security is the Nation's basic method of providing a continuing income when family earnings are reduced or stop because of retirement, disability, or death.

Nine out of 10 workers in the United States are earning protection under social security.

Nearly 1 out of every 7 persons in this country receives monthly social security checks.

About 23.1 million people 65 and over, nearly all of the Nation's aged population, have health insurance under Medicare. Another 2.6 million disabled people under 65 also have Medicare.

Nearly every family, then, has a stake in social security.

Changes Through the Years

Through the years since social security was enacted in 1935, there have been many changes to improve the protection it gives to workers and their families. At first, social security covered only the worker upon retirement; but in 1939, the law was changed to pay survivors when the worker died, as well as certain dependents when the worker retired.

Social security covered only workers in industry and commerce when the program began. In the 1950's, coverage was extended to include most self-employed persons, most State and local employees, household and farm employees, members of the Armed Forces, and members of the clergy. Today, almost all jobs in the United States are covered by social security.

Disability insurance benefits were first paid for July 1957, giving workers protection against loss of earnings due to total disability.

The social security program was expanded again in 1965 with the enactment of Medicare which assured hospital and medical insurance protection to people 65 and over. Since 1973, Medicare coverage has been available to people under 65 who have been entitled to disability checks for 2 or more consecutive years and to people with permanent kidney failure who need dialysis or kidney transplants.

As a result of legislation enacted in 1972, social security benefits will increase automatically in the future as the cost of living goes up.

Legislation enacted in late 1977 made an important change in the way benefits are calculated, restored the financial soundness of the social security program, and made other changes in the program...

Who Gets Checks?

Who gets a monthly social security check? The question can be answered in one word. People. All kinds of people. Young people, old people, poor people, rich people. Men, women, and children.

Monthly social security checks may go to workers and their dependents when the worker retires, becomes severely disabled, or dies. Then, there's Medicare, which helps pay the cost of health care for eligible people who are 65 or over or disabled.

Monthly benefits social security pays include:

Retirement checks — When you retire, you can start getting retirement checks as early as 62.

Disability checks — A worker who becomes severely disabled before 65 can get disability checks.

Under social security, you're considered disabled if you have a severe physical or mental condition which: prevents you from working, and is expected to last (or has lasted) for at least 12 months, or is expected to result in death.

Your checks can start for the 6th full month of your disability. Once checks start, they'll continue as long as you are disabled. If you are severely disabled, you could get benefits even though you manage to work a little.

Survivors checks — If the worker dies, survivors checks can go to certain members of the worker's family. A lump-sum payment also can be made when a worker dies. This payment usually goes to the widow or widower...

Medicare

The two parts of Medicare — hospital insurance and medical insurance — help protect people 65 and over from the high costs of health care. Also eligible for Medicare are disabled people under 65 who have been entitled to social security disability benefits for 24 or more consecutive months (including adults who are receiving benefits because they have been disabled since childhood). Insured workers and their dependents who need dialysis treatment or a kidney transplant because of permanent kidney failure also have Medicare protection.

The hospital insurance part of Medicare helps pay the cost of inpatient hospital care and certain kinds of followup care. The medical insurance part of Medicare helps pay the costs of physicians' services, outpatient hospital services, and for certain other medical items and services not covered by hospital insurance. People who have medical insurance pay a monthly premium. More than 70 percent of the cost of medical insurance is paid from general revenues of the Federal Government. The basic premium is $8.20 for the 12-month period beginning July 1978.

If you're eligible for a social security or railroad retirement check either as a worker, dependent, or survivor, you automatically have hospital insurance protection when you're 65...

People 65 and over who haven't worked long enough to be

eligible for hospital insurance can get this protection by enrolling and paying a monthly premium just as they would for other health insurance...

How Social Security is Financed

The basic idea of social security is a simple one: During working years, employees, their employers, and self-employed people pay social security contributions. This money is used only to pay benefits to the more than 33 million people getting benefits and to pay administrative costs of the program. Then, when today's workers' earnings stop or are reduced because of retirement, death, or disability, benefits will be paid to them from contributions by people in covered employment and self-employment at that time. These benefits are intended to replace part of the earnings the family has lost.

Part of the contributions made goes for hospital insurance under Medicare so workers and their dependents will have help in paying their hospital bills when they become eligible for Medicare. The medical insurance part of Medicare is financed by premiums paid by the people who have enrolled for this protection and amounts contributed by the Federal Government.

Preserve Social Security

If Social Security did not exist in its present beneficent form, we should have had to invent it. It must be preserved intact.

Charles Owen Rice, *Catholic Bulletin,* June 5, 1981.

If you're employed, you and your employer each pay an equal share of social security contributions. If you're self-employed, you pay contributions for retirement, survivors, and disability insurance at a rate about equal to 1½ times the employee rate. The hospital insurance contribution rate is the same for the employer, the employee, and the self-employed person.

As long as you have earnings that are covered by the law, you continue to pay contributions regardless of your age and even if you are receiving social security benefits...

Funds not required for current benefit payments and expenses are invested in interest-bearing U.S. Government securities.

The Government's share of the cost for supplemental medical insurance and certain other social security costs comes from general revenues of the U.S. Treasury, not from social security contributions.

"What nine out of ten working people are now doing is paying taxes to finance payments to persons who are not working."

Social Security Is Unfair

Milton and Rose Friedman

Milton Friedman is one of the leading and most influential defenders of traditional capitalism in the United States today. Nobel laureate economist (1976), *Newsweek* columnist and presidential adviser, he has authored several books including *Capitalism and Freedom*, *Price Theory* and *Dollars and Deficits*. The following viewpoint was taken from his book *Free To Choose*, written with his wife, Rose Friedman. In it, they attack social security as an unfair system which is being promoted "through misleading labeling and deceptive advertising."

Consider the following questions while reading:
1. What examples do the authors give to support their claim that social security has been promoted through "misleading labeling and deceptive advertising?"
2. According to the authors, what has caused social security's "long-run financial problems?"

The major welfare-state program in the United States on the federal level is Social Security — old age, survivors, disability, and health insurance...

Social Security and unemployment insurance were enacted in the 1930s to enable working people to provide for their own retirement and for temporary periods of unemployment rather than becoming objects of charity. Public assistance was introduced to aid persons in distress, with the expectation that it would be phased out as employment improved and as Social Security took over the task. Both programs started small. Both have grown like Topsy. Social Security has shown no sign of displacing public assistance — both are at all time highs in terms of both dollar expenditures and number of persons receiving payments. In 1978 payments under Social Security for retirement, disability, unemployment, hospital and medical care, and to survivors totaled more than $130 billion and were made to more than 40 million recipients...

To keep the discussion within manageable limits, we shall restrict this section to the major component of Social Security — old age and survivors' benefits, which accounted for nearly two-thirds of total expenditures and three-quarters of the recipients...

Deception of the Public

Social Security was enacted in the 1930s and has been promoted ever since through misleading labeling and deceptive advertising. A private enterprise that engaged in such labeling and advertising would doubtless be severely castigated by the Federal Trade Commission.

Consider the following paragraph that appeared year after year until 1977 in millions of copies of an unsigned HEW booklet entitled *Your Social Security:* "The basic idea of social security is a simple one: During working years employees, their employers, and self-employed people pay social security contributions which are pooled into special trust funds. When earnings stop or are reduced because the worker retires, becomes disabled, or dies, monthly cash benefits are paid to replace part of the earnings the family has lost."

This is Orwellian doublethink.

Payroll taxes are labeled "contributions" (or, as the Party might have put it in the book *Nineteen Eighty-four*, "Compulsory is Voluntary")...

The impression is given that a worker's "benefits" are financed by his "contributions." The fact is that taxes collected from persons at work were used to pay benefits to persons who had retired or to their dependents and survivors. No trust fund in any meaningful sense was being accumulated ("I am You").

Workers paying taxes today can derive no assurance from trust funds that they will receive benefits when they retire. Any assurance derives solely from the willingness of future taxpayers to impose taxes on themselves to pay for benefits that present taxpayers are promising themselves. This one-sided "compact between the generations," foisted on generations that cannot give their consent, is a very different thing from a "trust fund." It is more like a chain letter.

More Doublethink

The HEW booklets, including those currently being distributed also say, "Nine out of ten working people in the United States are earning protection for themselves and their families under the social security program."

More doublethink. What nine out of ten working people are now doing is paying taxes to finance payments to persons who are not working. The individual worker is not "earning" protection for himself and his family in the sense in which a person who contributes to a private vested pension system can be said to be "earning" his own protection. He is only "earning" protection in the political sense of satisfying certain administrative requirements for qualifying for benefits. Persons who now receive payments get much more than the actuarial value of the taxes that they paid and that were paid on their behalf. Young persons who now pay Social Security taxes are being promised much less than the actuarial value of the taxes that they will pay and that will be paid on their behalf.

Social Security is in no sense an insurance program in which individual payments purchase equivalent actuarial benefits. As even its strongest supporters admit, "The relationship between individual contributions (that is, payroll taxes) and benefits received is extremely tenuous." Social Security is, rather, a combination of a particular tax and a particular program of transfer payments.

The fascinating thing is that we have never met anyone, whatever his political persuasion, who would defend either the tax system by itself or the benefit system by itself. Had the two components been considered separately, neither would ever have been adopted!

Consider the tax. Except for a recent minor modification (rebates under the earned income credit), it is a flat rate on wages up to a maximum, a tax that is regressive, bearing most heavily on persons with low incomes. It is a tax on work, which discourages employers from hiring workers and discourages people from seeking work.

A Matter of Chance

Consider the benefit arrangement. Payments are determined neither by the amount paid by the beneficiary nor by his financial status. They constitute neither a fair return for prior payments nor an effective way of helping the indigent. There is a link between taxes paid and benefits received, but that is at best a fig leaf to give some semblance of credibility to calling the combination "insurance." The amount of money a person gets depends on all sorts of adventitious circumstances. If he happened to work in a covered industry, he gets a benefit; if he happened to work in a noncovered industry, he does not. If he worked in a covered industry for only a few quarters, he gets nothing, no matter how indigent he may be. A woman who has never worked, but is the wife or widow of a man who qualifies for the maximum benefit, gets precisely the same amount as a similarly situated woman who, in addition, qualifies for benefits on the basis of her own earnings. A person over sixty-five who decides to work and who earns more than a modest amount a year not only gets no benefits but, to add insult to injury, must pay additional taxes — supposedly to finance the benefits that are not being paid. And this list could be extended indefinitely...

The long-run financial problems of Social Security stem from one simple fact: the number of people receiving payments from the system has increased and will continue to increase faster than the number of workers on whose wages taxes can be levied to finance those payments. In 1950 seventeen persons were employed for every person receiving benefits; by 1970 only three; by early in the twenty-first century, if present trends continue, at most two will be.

Reprinted by permission of Don Wright, *The Miami News*.

Unfair Transfers

As these remarks indicate, the Social Security program involves a transfer from the young to the old. To some extent such a transfer has occurred throughout history — the young supporting their parents, or other relatives, in old age. Indeed, in many poor countries with high infant death rates, like India, the desire to assure oneself of progeny who can provide support in old age is a major reason for high birth rates and large families. The difference between Social Security and earlier arrangements is that Social Security is compulsory and impersonal — earlier arrangements were voluntary and personal. Moral responsibility is an individual matter, not a social matter. Children helped their parents out of love or duty. They now contribute to the support of someone else's parents out of compulsion and fear. The earlier transfers strengthened the bonds of the family; the compulsory transfers weaken them.

In addition to the transfer from young to old, Social Security also involves a transfer from the less well-off to the better-off. True, the benefit schedule is biased in favor of persons with lower wages, but this effect is much more than offset by another. Children from poor families tend to start work — and start paying employment taxes — at a relatively early age; children from higher income families at a much later age. At the other end of the life cycle, persons with lower incomes on the average have a shorter life span than persons with higher incomes. The net result is that the poor tend to pay taxes for more years and receive benefits for fewer years than the rich — all in the name of helping the poor...

All in all, Social Security is an excellent example of Director's Law in operation, namely, "Public expenditures are made for the primary benefit of the middle class, and financed with taxes which are borne in considerable part by the poor and rich."

"Social security is...a guaranteed real-income program for the general good...Congress should be making social security mandatory and universal."

Social Security Should Be Mandatory

Jane Bryant Quinn

Jane Bryant Quinn received her BA in journalism from Middlebury College (1960). The author of *Everyone's Money Book* (1978) and *Updated Everyone's Money Book* (1980), she has held numerous positions including syndicated financial columnist for the Washington Post Writers Group and most recently, columnist for *Newsweek* magazine. In the following viewpoint, she explains why she believes that social security is a "guaranteed real-income program for the general good" and concludes that it should be "mandatory and universal."

Consider the following questions while reading:
1. What examples does Ms. Quinn offer to counter the argument that social security costs too much?
2. How does the author respond to the argument that private annuities would provide a better retirement than social security?
3. According to Ms. Quinn, how could Congress strengthen social security?

Ugly suspicion and resentment are building up against the social-security system. The plaint runs something like this: "It's an expensive waste. I'd do better investing my money somewhere else. Besides, how do I know that social security won't go broke?"

This kind of thinking, plus high peeve against the Federal government, recently led employees of the State of Alaska to jettison social security in favor of a private system designed for them by the pension consulting firm William M. Mercer, Inc. Employees of private companies aren't allowed to jump ship, but participation remains voluntary for state and local governments and employees of non-profit institutions. In the past twenty years, 674 municipal groups, representing 111,988 employees, have actually pulled out; 222 more withdrawal notices are pending.

On the other hand, 120 withdrawal notices have themselves been withdrawn in the past three years, as employees rethink the surprising implications of life on the outside. A dropout vote is irrevocable; yet according to the Wyatt Co., a pension consulting firm, most groups that leave "have done so after superficial and incomplete analyses of the real issues."

Some Real Examples

• During New York City's financial crisis, the mayor announced that the city could save up to $250 million a year by pulling out of social security. On closer examination, a commission found that the city would actually have to pay $60 million *more* than the price of social security to self-insure for the same benefits.

• A 1977 study by the Commission on California State Government Organization and Economy found it would cost 28 per cent of payroll to approximate social-security benefits in the private market, as against an 11.7 per cent tag for social security itself.

• Mercer's 1976 study for Alaska put the cost of replacing most, but not all, of social security's benefits at 22 per cent of payroll, versus 10 per cent for social security. The plan actually adopted costs the same today as social security, but yields less.

A good many people are encouraged in their delusions about social security by phony calculations "proving" that if young people put the same money into a private annuity, they'd do better at retirement. But that approach ignores all the other benefits the system provides. For the same money, you get disability pay if you can't work, medicare, and payments to a dependent spouse, children and parents if you die. Depending on what happens in your life, you may draw very little on social security, or may get your money out many times over.

Some aspects of social security cannot be replaced at any

price. All social-security income is tax-exempt; you don't lose your right to payments if you leave the job after just a few years, as you do with most private pensions; benefits rise every year with the cost of living, so your purchasing power won't fall behind. "If a high, sustained inflation rate continues in the U.S.," says Mercer's A. Haeworth Robertson, "anyone opting out of social security will be sorry."

Social Security For All

Make Social Security a universal system. That means bringing into the system those public employees who are not covered by it and do not contribute to it. A universal system would spread the costs to more people, and probably permit a lowering of the payroll tax.

Harold Chucker, *The Minneapolis Star*, July 10, 1981.

The municipal workers most opposed to social security tend to be police and fire fighters, whose pensions are better than those of non-uniformed workers; working wives who have social-security coverage through husbands in private employment; young, well-paid workers who aren't yet thinking about the future and who may pick up social security in private employment later in life. In Alaska, fewer than half of the eligible employees voted. In consequence, 25 per cent of the workers determined the financial security of everyone else.

Two Telling Questions

The question for Congress is this: should employees who have security from other sources, or who bear a grudge against the government, be allowed to eliminate social insurance for people less fortunately placed? And, in view of the tragedy of the 1930s, can even higher-income people be dead sure that they will always be able to provide for themselves? The solid support for social security in Washington assures the long-term solvency of the system — if necessary, through general income-tax revenues. By contrast, city and company pensions, and private savings, are far more vulnerable to circumstance.

Social security isn't insurance. It's a guaranteed real-income program for the general good. Today's dropouts endanger the system's financing; yet someday they may themselves become wards of welfare because their own savings, insurance and disability aren't enough. Instead of allowing withdrawals, Congress should be making social security mandatory and universal.

> *"Social security must be reformed down to its roots or it will impoverish us all."*

Social Security Should Be Abandoned

Gary Allen

Gary Allen is a contributing editor of *American Opinion*, a monthly magazine published by Robert Welch, Inc. He is a conservative writer who authored the famous expose, *None Dare Call It Conspiracy*. His other books include *The Rockefeller File*, *Kissinger*, *Jimmy Carter/Jimmy Carter*, *Tax Target*, *Washington* and *Ted Kennedy: In Over His Head*. In the following viewpoint, he claims that unless the social security system is radically changed, it will soon be bankrupt and with it, millions of Americans.

Consider the following questions while reading:
1. According to Mr. Allen, why are social security payroll taxes creating a burden on American workers?
2. According to the author, what myths has the government created about social security?

Gary Allen, "What You Should Know about Social Security," *American Opinion*, March, 1981. Reprinted by permission of American Opinion Magazine.

The very words Social Security sound so reassuring that they could almost be included with motherhood, apple pie, baseball, and Chevrolet. But even this most soothing of "Liberal" phrases has begun to lose its magic power. Discussions of Social Security are now likely to be characterized by anxiety concerning its financial crises and the increasingly deep bites it is taking from the earnings of some 114 million workers now paying Social Security payroll taxes to provide benefits for 36 million recipients.

In 1960, the maximum amount of tax per worker paid to Social Security was $144 a year. Ten years later, in 1970, it had risen to $405 annually. In accordance with legislation passed by Congress in 1977, payroll taxes for Social Security took an enormous bound on January first of this year (1981). Wage earners are now being taxed at the rate of 6.65 percent on the first $29,700 of their annual wages. This amounts to a maximum tax of $1,975 this year...

An Unbearable Burden

Indeed, the Social Security tax is scheduled to be increased dramatically by stages every year through 1990.

An examiniation of the table here reveals how alarming this burden on American workers is to become...

YEAR	MAXIMUM COVERED WAGE	TAX RATE	MAXIMUM AMOUNT OF TAX
1980	$25,900	6.13%	$1,588
1981	$29,700	6.65%	$1,975
1982	$32,700	6.70%	$2,191
1983	$35,700	6.70%	$2,392
1984	$39,600	6.70%	$2,653
1985	$43,500	7.05%	$3,067
1986	$47,700	7.15%	$3,411
1987	$51,900	7.15%	$3,711
1988	$56,400	7.15%	$4,033
1989	$61,500	7.15%	$4,397
1990	$66,900	7.65%	$5,118

These taxes are escalating so fast that revenues for Social Security are now expected to equal one fourth of all federal Budget receipts this year, up from less than twenty percent in 1970, and less than ten percent in 1955. More than half of all American families now pay more in Social Security taxes than they do in federal income taxes...

Because people are living longer, retiring earlier, having fewer children, experiencing increased joblessness, and being victimized by inflation, old age and survivor outlays have grown like the creature that ate Cleveland and there will be fewer people in the work force to bear this increasing burden.

In 1960, for everyone receiving Social Security benefits there were five workers paying Social Security taxes. Today, there are about three persons paying the taxes to support one beneficiary. By the time the young people entering jobs today retire, there could be as many as sixty-three beneficiaries for every one hundred workers — or only about 1.6 workers per beneficiary. The burden will thus grow heavier and heavier for those still employed in the work force.

Pyramid Scheme is Not Insurance

Obviously the biggest myth behind the Social Security pyramid scheme is the notion that it is an "insurance" program. This false notion has been encouraged by millions of pieces of literature put out by the Social Security Administration containing misleading and false statements. Thus many people view the Social Security payroll tax as a "premium" for a government-run insurance program; they see Social Security benefits as something they've paid for and are entitled to upon retirement. Many naively believe that their "contributions" go into a "trust fund" account with their name on it and that they will receive benefits according to their payments when they retire. Unfortunately, that is not so.

Social Security Pays Less

If young workers were allowed to save and invest in a tax-free retirement account the amounts they would otherwise pay in Social Security taxes, they could earn far greater retirement benefits than they are currently promised under Social Security. And because of the financing problems of Social Security, it is unlikely that even the promised benefits will ever be paid.

Peter J. Ferrara, *Human Events*, September 5, 1981.

When the question of Social Security's constitutionality was raised before the Supreme Court in 1937, the Social Security lawyers admitted to the Court that it was not insurance but a Welfare plan, saying: "Moreover, the Act creates no contractual obligation with respect to the payment of benefits. The court has pointed out the difference between insurance, which creates vested interests, and pensions and other gratuities involving no contractual obligations. The Act cannot be said to constitute a plan for compulsory insurance within the accepted meaning of the term 'insurance.' "

The so-called "trust funds" contain no cash, but only bonds — pieces of paper signed by politicians representing promises to pay in the future. The money taken from millions of people for Social Security has already been spent by the government. It's gone. The promise that you will get something out of the program later when you retire relies entirely on the government's power to tax the next generation to its knees...

The government securities residing in the Social Security "trust funds" represent a colossal debt to be paid by and by. And these mounting debts must somehow, some way, be paid as workers reach advanced age. They aren't likely to be.

Meanwhile, practically nobody understands how the system works. Nobody is *supposed* to understand. The idea is to keep the American people in the dark and confused about the actual nature of the Social Security scheme so they will trust the politicians in Washington. In fact, *Barron's* quotes an obviously anonymous Social Security official as admitting: "Continued general support for the Social Security system hinges on continued public ignorance of how the system works. I believe that we have nothing to worry about because it is so enormously complex that nobody is going to figure it out."...

Bureaucrats Know Better

Social Security differs from other pyramid schemes only in its giant proportions and the fact that unlike a chain-letter game it is a compulsory rather than a voluntary venture. Even if you don't want to play the Social Security game, and even if you have made other provisions for your retirement years, you are required to pay the F.I.C.A. taxes now being spent...

That the politicians and bureaucrats know something is very wrong with Social Security is indicated by the fact that they arranged carefully to exempt themselves from it. The politicians and government administrators who have arranged Social Security for the rest of us are not about to settle for a subsistence retirement...

There are assuredly countless savings plans and insurance programs which outperform Social Security to provide a much greater nest egg by age sixty-five. A person might enroll in such programs now, but if he does so he must pay for them *in addition to* what he is already forced to pay Social Security. Most cannot afford to do both. Besides, a citizen might not want to save for his old age at all, preferring to stake every penny on a business enterprise which requires capital goods in the present but will provide amply for the investor's old age. The government doesn't give us this option. And since everything that one is made to pay into the Social Security system is forfeited to the government, one cannot draw a cent of it for investment purposes during his younger years. Instead, we are taxed heavily by this program just when we need the money most to provide for current needs. The whole thing is as nonsensical as it is destructive.

Welfare Characteristics of Social Security

Not that this scam has anything to do with good sense. The Welfare characteristic of Social Security becomes even more obvious when we observe that the amount of benefits one may receive depends on factors other than the amount of one's "contributions" to the system — factors such as marital status, sex, and the amount of income one receives from other sources. For instance, a married woman is entitled to receive benefits as a dependent of her husband if he is on Social Security. But, if she has been working and contributing to the system for years she will get no more than if she had never worked outside the home at all. That is, she will get the same amount as a wife who never paid Social Security taxes from her salary...

In contrast with the Social Security ripoff, a 21-year-old man working at an average salary could purchase an insurance policy that would give him a much better retirement income if he were free to invest the money which he is now required to pay into the government system. A young worker who earns at least $29,700 in wages is paying $1,975 a year to Social Security. He could pay *nothing* until he is thirty-five and still take out a private policy that would provide him with more than Social Security — if he were free annually to invest that $1,975 instead of losing it forever in taxes. And, remember, this does not include his boss's matching "contribution."

Effect on the Economy

Compounding the problem is the tremendously negative effect Social Security has had on the American economy. The system seriously discourages private saving and investment, drastically reducing America's capital accumulation. Productivity, economic growth, and the general standard of living all depend, in the long run, on capital formation resulting from saving and investment...Our productivity has been declining in recent years, and our economy has experienced much slower economic growth than it once did. No one knows how much higher our standard of living would be today had the American people been permitted to keep, save, and invest the money they were forced to throw down the federal rathole into Social Security. This is because no one can accurately predict how much of their money people would save or spend if free to do so. It has been calculated however that if the aggregate savings of the U.S. economy are reduced by the full amount of Social Security taxes, then private savings for 1979 were reduced by about forty-five percent. Even if we assume that Social Security takes away from private savings only thirty-five percent, it means that the G.N.P. in 1979 was decreased by more than $450 *billion* because of the Social Security program alone. The loss in production, economic growth, job creation, and national income is simply enormous...

As advanced as the problem has become, there is no painless solution to the Social Security dilemma. The system must

Reprinted with permission of the *Minneapolis Tribune*.

be reformed down to its roots or it will impoverish us all. Such reform should assure that current retirees are not short-changed. At the same time, it should provide incentives for younger workers to invest in private alternatives which, in time, would stimulate production and jobs by infusions of new capital into the economy.

"A significant percentage of older persons are hovering just above the officially defined poverty line."

The Elderly Need Social Security

Cyril F. Brickfield

Cyril F. Brickfield is Executive Director of the National Retired Teachers Association and the American Association of Retired Persons, the nation's oldest and largest organizations of older Americans. An attorney and former professor of Constitutional law at Catholic University, he is the author of a number of monographs dealing with domestic and international law. In the following viewpoint, Mr. Brickfield directs the reader's attention to the financial plight of the elderly by asserting that millions of retired persons do not enjoy an adequate retirement income.

Consider the following questions while reading:
1. What two myths concerning the elderly does Mr. Brickfield object to and why does he object?
2. Why does the author believe that regressive proposals to alter social security will result in economic disaster for older Americans?

Fifteen years ago, they were eating dog food. Today, they are affluent and living well. For the nation's nearly 25,000,000 older citizens, a remarkable economic transformation has taken place since the 1960's. Or has it?

It is true that older Americans had serious economic problems in the 1960's. Their poverty rate was appallingly high. Social Security benefit increases — subject to the whims of Congress — were few and far between, and Medicare and Medicaid did not even come into existence until 1966.

However, the reports that surfaced in those years of older persons eating dog food were apparently myths that could never be corroborated. (I always wondered why an old man or woman would resort to eating dog food when the price of such things as chicken was actually cheaper.)

The New Myth Concerning the Elderly

Now, in the 1980's, it seems that the pendulum has swung completely the other way. We've discovered a brand new myth about the elderly. In recent months, we've seen a proliferation of newspaper stories, magazine columns, and statements by public officials and other so-called "experts" — all stressing the theme that older Americans are generally living quite well despite the continuing presence of double-digit inflation during the past several years.

Some of these writers take great pains to cite examples of well-heeled elders buying posh condominiums, piloting sailboats, and making huge profits in the stock market. They then use these exceptional cases to justify their claims that the elderly are doing just fine...

Others cite statistics showing a significant drop in the poverty rate among the elderly since the early 1970's, but fail to point out that there is a considerable difference between escaping poverty and living comfortably, let alone affluently. They ignore the critical question of how many older Americans have *adequate* retirement income. The answer is that millions do not. More that 58% of all elderly single persons and 36% of elderly couples do *not* have sufficient cash and in-kind income (Medicare, food stamps, etc.) to attain what the government defines as a moderate standard of retirement living (approximately $6,500 for single persons and $9,800 for couples).

The fact is that a significant percentage of older persons are hovering just above the officially defined poverty line. Those who advocate a reduction in benefits to the elderly fail to recognize that a reduction of only $25 per week per person would increase the rate of poverty among the nation's elderly to at least 25%, higher than it was during the 1960's.

Poverty Rates Among Elderly are Increasing

The latest available statistics show that the poverty rate

among the elderly has already started increasing again. During 1979, the elderly poverty rate rose from 14% to 15.1%, meaning that 400,000 additional older persons fell into poverty that year. The near-poverty rate for the elderly (defined as 125% of the poverty threshold) increased during the same period from 23.4% to 24.7%. In contrast, poverty and near-poverty rates for the general population rose only slightly during 1979.

Normally, I would welcome the efforts of those who are trying to correct the commonly held misconception that *most* elderly people are living in abject poverty and that they are invariably frail, helpless, and immobile. After all, those of us in the field of aging have fought for years to show society that millions of older persons are reasonably healthy and active and are still able to constructively participate in every aspect of American life.

Unfortunately, these new mythmakers go too far. Rather than merely debunking old stereotypes, they are creating new ones. They are implying that, because the elderly were able to make significant economic progress during the 1970's, older persons can now afford to give up some cost-of-living increases in Social Security benefits, to have the entitlement date for receiving these benefits postponed, or to pay taxes on all or part of them.

These myths are generating increased distrust, jealousy, and conflict between generations. They are spawning a number of regressive proposals to alter the Social Security System. Worst of all, they are setting the stage for possible economic disaster for millions of older Americans...

Primarily in order to alleviate the intolerable rate of poverty among the elderly during the 1960's, Congress mandated several significant increases in Social Security benefits from 1968 to 1972, culminating with a 20% increase in 1972. It should be obvious that such dramatic increases in benefits are unlikely to occur again. At the same time, continued overall price increases, led by the sharp escalation of energy and health care costs, will continue to pose a greater burden for the elderly than for the non-elderly...

Based upon these economic forecasts, I am convinced that some of the proposals to change the Social Security System that are now being discussed in Washington would be nothing less than catastrophic for millions of Americans.

For example, both the Reagan Administration and several members of Congress have proposed a variety of significant changes in Social Security, including raising the normal entitlement age for benefits from 65 to 68, altering the benefit formula for new retirees, and using an index lower than the CPI (Consumer Price Index) to adjust benefits after retirement.

These proposals are, in my view, very shortsighted.

Raising the entitlement age would substantially reduce and in some cases eliminate benefits for many older persons who are involuntarily unemployed or physically unable to work. It also would destroy what remains of younger workers' confidence in the future solvency and stability of the Social Security System. With all of the talk about the financial problems plaguing Social Security, postponing the date on which younger workers would receive their benefits would be — in their eyes — merely a prelude to their losing the benefits altogether because of the system's inability to pay them.

Changes Must Be Positive to Prevent Catastrophe

Rather than forcing older persons to work longer and depriving them of a choice, the government should institute positive incentives for them to continue working, such as delayed retirement bonuses and elimination of the Social Security earnings test.

Moreover, at a time when inflation is rapidly eroding the fixed incomes of millions of Americans, it would be criminal to cut back on the only inflation protection they have by using a lower index than the CPI. Most significantly, the suggested changes in the benefit computation formula for new retirees would reduce benefits for future retirees by as much as 50% in some cases.

Social Security A Must

Most Americans depend on Social Security to provide a basic floor of protection to replace income lost because of retirement, disability or death. They rely on Social Security to work together with their company pensions and savings to provide them with adequate financial security.

Gary Taylor, *Shell News*, February, 1982.

Since at least 60% of all older persons depend on Social Security for the majority of their income, proposals like these could well mean poverty and totally inadequate standards of living not only for today's older Americans, but for large numbers of the future elderly population as well.

This is not to argue that we should do nothing to change the Social Security System. To the contrary, it is obvious that economic and demographic pressures will make it impossible to continue the present system into the next century. Without a major and comprehensive restructuring of that system, older Americans in the future may not be able to rely on it as the major source of their income.

We must not ignore the very real need for reform of our nation's private pension policies. As the President's Commis-

sion on Pension Policy noted in its interim report: "the existence of one other pension benefit often was the difference between poverty and non-poverty." Surely, within the next 10 years, the nation is going to have to develop a mechanism such as the universal minimum mandatory pension system proposed by the President's Commission. Without it, the demographic impact of a larger retirement population and a smaller workforce will result in the collapse of our whole income support structure for older Americans.

I foresee disastrous consequences in the years to come if the nation's policy- and opinion-makers base changes in Social Security and private pensions on false assumptions about the future economic condition of older persons.

To argue that older Americans are living well enough as a class to endure any significant reduction in benefits is to ignore the somber economic prognosis for them during this decade.

"It's time to ask not have we done enough for the elderly, but have we done too much?"

The Elderly May Not Need Social Security

Joan Beck

Joan Beck, currently a writer for the *Chicago Tribune*, received both a BS and MS in journalism from Northwestern University. She has authored several books including *Is My Baby Alright?* and *Effective Parenting.* In the following viewpoint, Ms. Beck addresses herself to the question of social security being essentially a "transfer" program in which the young of society are supporting the old. She concludes by challenging the wisdom and fairness of the program.

Consider the following questions while reading:

1. What does Ms. Beck say will happen to force reassessments of "intergenerational income transfers?"
2. According to Ann Kutza, what is wrong with income transfer programs and why do the truly needy often lose out?
3. What arguments for continued support of current programs does the author agree are good arguments?

Joan Beck, "Do Elderly Really Need All that Social Security?" *St. Paul Pioneer Press*, August 10, 1981. Reprinted by permission of Tribune Company Syndicate, Inc.

You and your spouse both work. You have two preschoolers in day care that cost you a bundle. Your car's a 6-year-old clunker. You have a chunk of credit card debts. And you have no prospects whatever of financing a house.

Why should you have to transfer some of your income to a 66-year-old couple with a paid-up mortgage, good health, good health insurance, a pension that pays about half of their last working year's salary, decreasing financial responsibilities and a few investments on the side?

Few people are looking at benefit programs for the elderly in quite this way yet...

Imbalance Between Young and Old

But the time may come soon when the increasing imbalance between the numbers of the young and the elderly and the rapidly growing size of intergenerational income transfers will force some sharp reassessments.

Age may turn out not to be an appropriate reason for giving part of the population an entitlement to tax money, argues Elizabeth Ann Kutza of the University of Chicago in a new book, "The Benefits of Old Age" (University of Chicago Press).

Yet we have locked ourselves into such a confusing proliferation of income transfer programs based on age that the elderly — who make up 11 percent of the population — now get one dollar out of every four in the federal budget for fiscal 1981.

That's up 30 percent from 1979. And the totals will keep increasing, along with the growing number of those over 65.

It is true that some elderly people need financial help, says Kutza. But only 14 percent of the elderly fall below federal poverty lines (most likely single women living alone) compared to 11.6 percent in the population. And this definition of "poverty" doesn't count non-cash benefits, such as food stamps or Medicare.

About 5 million elderly — one in every four — get benefits from three or more federal programs, according to Kutza. Ninety percent collect from two or more.

Truly Needy Often Get Lost

Yet some people still slip through this hodge-podge of help to remain poor not only because the benefits from one program may be subtracted from entitlements from another but because the truly needy get lost in the shuffle of benefits that aren't targeted for them but given out wholesale on the basis of age alone.

"Chronological age is not a good indicator of an individual's circumstances," notes Kutza..."No problem occurs in old age that does not occur in other age groups, whether it be poverty, mental or physical disability, isolation or malnutrition."

A larger percent of the young (aged 5 to 17) live in poverty than of the elderly.

Almost as many non-elderly (3.3 million) have chronic health problems that keep them from working as do the old (3.8 million). Many of the elderly, especially the "young-old" between 65 and 75, are taking up second careers, going to school, enjoying vigorous sports.

Nine percent of all families in the United States with incomes greater than $50,000 are headed by someone older than 65.

In fact, chronological age may no longer be a useful way to organize work and social patterns for a society — or for individuals, suggest Kutza and others.

Arguments for Continued Support

There are good arguments for continuing to support the elderly in the income-transfer style to which the government has encouraged them to become accustomed. Retirement rules prevent many who are vigorous and capable from working. Some are unable to support themselves. Many in dead-end, routine jobs are eager for leisure.

Let's Be Fair

The standards of living of the elderly cannot rise while those of the rest of the country fall. That is no longer fair or economically feasible.

Lester C. Thurow, *Newsweek*, May 24, 1982.

Families would have to support some of the elderly if the government didn't, and might find the burden unbearable. The elderly who truly need help — perhaps after a lifetime of earning their own way — find it easier to take if it's called an entitlement or insurance rather than welfare.

And all of the rhetoric about Social Security has led the public to think of it as insurance that they are buying, instead of the inter-generational income transfer plan that it is.

The pension aspects of Social Security aren't going to change; politics makes that impossible. Neither will Medicare. But as other age-based entitlement programs grow, as the number of elderly increases, as tax burdens and financial pressures on young adults mount, and as costs soar, it's time to ask, says Kutza, "not have we done enough for the elderly, but have we done too much?"

Distinguishing Bias
From Reason

The subject of state welfarism often generates great emotional responses in people. When dealing with such a highly cntroversial subject, many will allow their feelings to dominate their powers of reason. Thus, one of the most important basic thinking skills is the ability to distinguish between opinions based upon emotion or bias and conclusions based upon a rational consideration of the facts.

Most of the following statements are taken from the viewpoints in this chapter. The rest are taken from other sources. Consider each statement carefully. *Mark R for any statement you believe is based on reason or a rational consideration of the facts. Mark B for any statement you believe is based on bias, prejudice or emotion. Mark I for any statement you think is impossible to judge.*

If you are doing this activity as the member of a class or group compare your answers with those of other class or group members. Be able to defend your answers. You may discover that others will come to different conclusions than you. Listening to the rationale others present for their answers may give you valuable insights in distinguishing between bias and reason.

If you are reading this book alone, ask others if they agree with your answers. You too will find this interaction very valuable.

> *R = a statement based on reason*
> *B = a statement based on bias*
> *I = a statement impossible to judge*

1. The fact is that social security taxes collected from persons at work are used to pay benefits to persons who have retired or to their dependents and survivors.

2. Children from poor families tend to start work at a relatively early age; children from higher income families at a much later age.

3. Some aspects of social security cannot be replaced at any price.

4. The municipal workers most opposed to social security tend to be police and fire fighters, whose pensions are better than those of non-uniformed workers.

5. Because of the financing problems of social security, it is unlikely that even the promised benefits will ever be paid.

6. The idea is to keep the American people in the dark and confused about the actual nature of the social security scheme so they will trust the politicians in Washington.

7. Social security differs from other pyramid schemes only in its giant proportions and the fact that unlike a chain-letter game it is a compulsory rather than a voluntary venture.

8. The social security system seriously discourages private saving and investment, drastically reducing America's capital accumulation.

9. Without social security, the demographic impact of a larger retirement population and a smaller workforce will result in the collapse of our whole income support structure for older Americans.

10. No problem occurs in old age that does not occur in other age groups, whether it be poverty, mental or physical disability, isolation or malnutrition.

11. If retired persons did not have the foresight to save for their retirement, the government should not be responsible for them.

12. It is the *moral duty* of all governments to care for their elderly citizens with public funds.

13. It is the *moral duty* of all families to personally care for their elderly members.

Bibliography

The following list of periodical articles deals with the subject matter of this chapter.

Business Week   "Battle Over Repairing Social Security," September 28, 1981, p. 116.

Changing Times   "How Safe Is the Social Security System?," July, 1979, p. 4.

Wilbur J. Cohen   "Threat to Social Security," *The New Leader*, June 1, 1981, p. 5.

Congressional Digest   "Financing Social Security," August 5, 1981, p. 195.

Donald A. Feder   "Social Security: Time To Cut Our Losses," *The Libertarian Review*, February, 1981, p. 12.

Peter J. Ferrara   "Social Security: How Much Longer Can It Last?" *The Libertarian Review*, February 1981, p. 18.

W. Flanagan   "How Uncle Screws Us All," *Esquire*, January 30, 1979, p. 79.

James M. Hildreth   "The Battle to Save Social Security," *U.S. News & World Report*, July 20, 1981, p. 41.

The Libertarian Review   "Social Security's Eleventh Hour," February, 1981, p. 2.

The Nation   "Social Insecurity," May 20, 1981, p. 651.

Newsweek   "Playing Politics with Social Security," July 20, 1981, p. 22.

Rita Ricardo-Campbell   "Social Security — New Directions," *Vital Speeches of the Day*, November 1, 1981, p. 52.

Rita Ricardo-Campbell vs. Betty Duskin   "Pro and Con: Raise Social Security Retirement Age?" *U.S. News & World Report*, July 27, 1981, p. 35.

Jeff Riggenback   "How Security Became Social," *The Libertarian Review*, February, 1981, p. 15.

Bradley R. Schiller   "A Supply-Side Approach to Social Security," *USA Today*, September, 1981, p. 15.

Miriam Schneir   "How Social Security Shortchanges Women," *McCalls*, June, 1981, p. 42.

Time   "A Debt-Threatened Dream," May 24, 1982, p. 16.

Lester C. Thurow   "Saving Social Security," *Newsweek*, October 26, 1981, p. 71.

Are There Alternatives
to Welfare?

**THE
WELFARE
STATE**

"To make the welfare program achieve its goals, the best alternative would seem to be that of the negative income tax."

Negative Income Tax Is the Best Alternative

Robert W. Haseltine

Robert W. Haseltine is Associate Professor of Economics at the School of Business, State University of New York, Geneseo. He received both his bachelor and master degrees from Northern Illinois University and has had additional graduate study in economics at Syracuse University. A Senior Economics Editor for the magazine *USA Today*, Mr. Haseltine is also Series Editor for the *Economic Information Guide* series published by Gale Research, Inc. In the following viewpoint, he explains why he believes that the negative income tax would offer the best alternative to America's "welfare mess."

Consider the following questions while reading:

1. Why does Mr. Haseltine believe that the welfare system is "a mess?"
2. Why does he believe that a negative income tax is the best alternative to the present welfare system?

Robert W. Haseltine, "Welfare Costs Vs. the Negative Income Tax." Reprinted from Intellect Magazine, October 1977. Copyright 1977 by Society for the Advancement of Education.

The welfare system of the U.S. is a mess. According to reports presented by various of the media, one out of every six
citizens of New York City is on welfare; there are more children
registered for welfare in New York City than there are children;
and, in Chicago, a "welfare queen" has been convicted on a
number of counts of fraud, with the allegation that these were
only a few of the many she had perpetrated. Yet, due to the
technicalities in the law, some people can not receive food
stamps because they are too poor to pay for them, or because
the county in which they reside does not accept the food stamp
program for its citizens.

The Welfare Mess

It would seem the welfare mess exists for a number of
reasons. Too many bureaus handle the problems of poverty,
with a resultant overlap of caseloads, and each gets in the
other's way as each does it own thing with little regard for the
final outcome. Those who are hurt are not the bureaucrats, for
they can not be faulted for doing what the law requires them to
do.

Welfare laws are themselves a hodgepodge (as are the tax
laws), for most have been instituted on an *ad hoc* basis over the
past 40·years to take care of the problems of poverty, but
wound up taking care of the symptoms. Even the alleviation of
the symptoms proved to be spotty, as money meant to help the
poor in their fight against unemployment and high prices
found its way into the salary checks of people who already
were beyond the need of welfare, but were hired to supervise
the programs...

Recent headlines make obvious that which has been
apparent, but has been glossed over by the statistician, as he
pointed out that only a small number of welfare recipients were
undeserving. There is no arguing with that fact. Unfortunately,
there is a reasonably large amount of money which is siphoned
off by this minority, as well as by high-salaried welfare co-
ordinators of the Federal programs. If welfare is the means of
accomplishing the goal of redistribution of income, in those
cases where the system maldistributes it, it is not doing its job.
An alternative method, which is less expensive and has a better
chance of reaching the low-income class at which it is aimed is
the negative income tax.

Problems Under the Welfare System

One of the first accomplishments of the implementation of a
negative income tax would be the abolishing of the plethora of
welfare agencies supported by the public — be they local,
state, or Federal. Abolishing these agencies would save a large
amount of tax dollars (which could be better used elsewhere)
above the actual amount disbursed for payments to low-

income recipients.

The crux of any change is to institute a system which will accomplish the goals of alleviating poverty in the U.S. at a minimum cost and which gives the maximum degree of fairness. Built into this system should be a method of making sure monies disbursed go to those who need it, to assure that incentives to work are built into the program, and to raise as many of the low-income population as possible from the sector which receives money from the government to that of one which pays money into the government.

"*I think I could have coped with wine, women and song, but then they threw pensions, welfare and medicare at me . . .*"

Reprinted with permission from the *Vancouver Sun.*

Under current welfare programs — as has been pointed out by the media — money is not always received by those who actually need it. Welfare fraud is endemic throughout the country, and some money is siphoned into the pockets of more affluent members of the community (not because of dishonesty, but because the law favors these people, rather than the lower-income group at which it is aimed). Much of the appropriated Federal money is used to run the agencies and pay the salaries of those who determine who gets what and how much what he gets...

The Negative Income Tax

In order to reduce the costs of welfare and to make the welfare program achieve its goals, the best alternative would seem to be that of the negative income tax. In essence, it would take the income level the government declares to be the poverty level, make this the minimum income for the country, and provide incentives for those earning less than this amount to attempt to rise to income levels above it. The one department that would feel the strain of this would be the Internal Revenue Service.

Since the Internal Revenue Service is computerized, receives information regarding income from businesses and banks, is capable of evaluating income tax returns filed by income earners, and income taxes are already instituted throughout the country, the implementation of the negative income tax would be relatively simple. Slight changes in the forms would have to be made, but changes seem to be made every year, so this should pose no difficulty.

All heads of families, or individuals above the age of 16 and not attending school (in addition to those who are now filing for the reasons of earning income and having to pay taxes), would have to file an income tax return. The individual with taxable income would be treated no differently than he is now — the difference would lie in the treatment of those making less than poverty levels of income.

Gross income and taxable income are different, so the same method of arriving at taxable income would be employed as it is at this time. In order to illustrate the operations of the tax, assume a family with a total of three dependents earning $5,000 during the year as a gross income figure.

If, by itemizing deductions, the family does not exceed the 15% allowed, they would take the 15%, or $750, and deduct it from the $5,000. Exemptions are claimed at $750 each, a total of $2,250, and this is now deducted from the $4,250 left after deductions are subtracted. Taxable income is $2,000. The poverty level of $5,500 exceeds taxable income by $3,500, so this deficit is indicated on the tax form. If we assume the percentage of payoff to be 75% of the difference between taxable income and poverty-level income — and this is an arbitrary figure subject to change — the family would receive a transfer payment from the government of $2,625. This could be paid on a monthly basis of $218.75 to supplement the monthly income during the next year. As is the case with most transfer payments, this money would be non-taxable.

Advantages of the Negative Income Tax

It would seem there are a number of advantages to the negative income tax system in relation to the current system of welfare. First, it would reduce the chance of welfare fraud, as W-2 forms can be more readily checked than can some of the information required on welfare applications. Second, only those who are really in need of assistance would get assistance. The tax forms would be an immediate check on those in need versus those above poverty level. This would mean, of course, that many payments would cease (such as soil bank payments or other crop payments giving the large landholder an advantage over the smaller landholder). Third, all of the existing forms of welfare could be eliminated — this would, in itself, save billions of dollars in costs of operations, paperwork, and salaries. Fourth, the actual goals of welfare, especially that of redistributing income to the proper recipients, would be realized.

"The various schemes for a guaranteed annual income are no genuine replacement for the universally acknowledged evils of the welfare system."

Negative Income Tax Is the Worst Alternative

Murray N. Rothbard

Murray N. Rothbard received his Ph.D. from Columbia University and is currently Professor of Economics at the Polytechnic Institute of New York. A member of the Libertarian National Committee and a leading voice in the national Libertarian movement, he has published countless articles supportive of the free enterprise system. His books include: *Conceived in Liberty, Man, Economy and State* and *America's Great Depression.* In the following viewpoint, Dr. Rothbard maintains that the negative income tax would ultimately prove a greater disaster than the current welfare system.

Consider the following questions while reading:
1. According to the author, what is the "one element that saves the present welfare system from being an utter disaster?" Do you agree?
2. Why does Mr. Rothbard feel that the guaranteed annual income will not replace the existing welfare system?

Reprinted with permission of Macmillan Publishing Co., Inc. from *For a New Liberty* by Murray N. Rothbard.

Unfortunately, the recent trend...is to abolish the current welfare system *not* in the direction of freedom but toward its very opposite. This new trend is the "guaranteed annual income" or "negative income tax..."

Citing the inefficiencies, inequities, and red tape of the present system, the guaranteed annual income would make the dole easy, "efficient," and automatic: The income tax authorities will pay money each year to families earning below a certain base income — this automatic dole to be financed, of course, by taxing working families making more than the base amount. Estimated costs of this seemingly neat and simple scheme are supposed to be only a few billion dollars per year.

A Wrong Assumption

But there is an extremely important catch: the costs are estimated *on the assumption* that everyone — the people on the universal dole as well as those financing it — will continue to work to the same extent as before. But this assumption begs the question. For the chief problem is the enormously crippling disincentive effect the guaranteed annual income will have on taxpayer and recipient alike.

The one element that saves the present welfare system from being an utter disaster is precisely the red tape and the stigma involved in going on welfare. The welfare recipient still bears a psychic stigma even though weakened in recent years, and he still has to face a typically inefficient, impersonal, and tangled bureaucracy. But the guaranteed annual income, *precisely* by making the dole efficient, easy, and automatic will remove the major obstacles, the major disincentives, to the "supply function" for welfare, and will lead to a massive flocking to the guaranteed dole. Moreover, everyone will now consider the new dole as an automatic "right" rather than as a privilege or gift, and all stigma will be removed.

No Incentive To Work

Suppose, for example, that $4,000 per year is declared the "poverty line," and that everyone earning income below that line receives the difference from Uncle Sam automatically as a result of filling out his income tax return. Those making zero income will receive $4,000 from the government, those making $3,000 will get $1,000, and so on. It seems clear that there will be no real reason for *anyone* making less than $4,000 a year to keep on working. Why should he, when his nonworking neighbor will wind up with the same income as himself? In short, the net income from working will then be zero, and the entire working population below the magic $4,000 line will quit work and flock to its "rightful" dole.

But this is not all; what of the people making either $4,000, or slightly or even moderately above that line? The man making

Murray N. Rothbard

$4,500 a year will soon find that the lazy slob next door who refuses to work will be getting his $4,000 a year from the federal government; his own net income from forty hours a week of hard work will be only $500 a year. So he will quit work and go on the negative-tax dole. The same will undoubtedly hold true for those making $5,000 a year, etc....

Additional Considerations

In addition to all this, there are some important extra considerations. In practice, of course, the dole, once set at $4,000, will not remain there; irresistible pressure by welfare clients and other pressure groups will inexorably raise the base level every year, thereby bringing a vicious spiral and economic disaster that much closer. In practice, too, the guaranteed annual income will *not*, as in the hopes of its conservative advocates, *replace* the existing patchwork welfare system; it will simply be added *on top of* the existing programs. This, for example, is precisely what happened to the states' old-age relief programs. The major talking point of the New Deal's federal Social Security program was that it would efficiently *replace* the then existing patchwork old-age relief programs of the states. In practice, of course, it did no such thing, and old-age relief is far higher now than it was in the 1930s. An ever-rising Social Security structure was simply placed on top of existing programs...

The various schemes for a guaranteed annual income are no genuine replacement for the universally acknowledged evils of the welfare system; they would only plunge us still more deeply into those evils.

> *"The graduated income supplement is designed to save tax dollars and, at the same time, to achieve the goal of public assistance."*

The "Graduated Income Supplement" Alternative

Leonard M. Greene

Leonard M. Greene is president of the Institute for Socioeconomic Studies, a Westchester, New York, think tank. He has served on the Panel on Welfare Reform with the United States Chamber of Commerce. An economist and mathematician, Mr. Greene was a research scientist during World War II and developed the first theory for sound barrier flight. In the following viewpoint, he proposes what he terms the "Graduated Income Supplement" as an alternative to the current welfare system. By providing for universal eligibility, he explains why the "supplement" would "eliminate the potential for abuse."

Consider the following questions while reading:
1. How would the Graduated Income Supplement work?
2. Why would the Graduated Income Supplement increase the incentive to work?
3. What is your opinion of the Graduated Income Supplement?

While we Americans are willing to help our destitute neighbors, we have no desire to support a dependent class permanently. Yet our welfare system has not abolished poverty, and it has actually led to increased dependency...

Despite the risks and perils, an effort must be made to replace welfare as we know it, before the present dependency system completely destroys the work incentive in our country and, because of the immense financial burden it puts on our economy, triggers violent upheaval.

A truly comprehensive plan for welfare reform must (a) include a work incentive; (b) promote the integrity of the family; (c) offer uniform benefits; (d) be integrated into our tax system; and (e) be easy to administer.

A Workable Proposal

I therefore propose the Graduated Income Supplement (GIS), a mechanism which will meet all of these requirements, with the strength of great simplicity.

Every adult and, at a different level, every child is to receive a taxable income supplement. The dollar value of that supplement will be reflected on the income tax return as a reduction of taxes owed. If the amount of taxes owed is less than the supplement, a cash refund will be made. A family with no income will receive the full amount of the supplement in cash payments. Because the supplement is taxable income, its net value is progressive in accordance with the graduated income tax.

The Graduated Income Supplement will not call for a determination of the assets or the need of recipients. Its basic payments will be unrelated to any financial standard. However, thanks to taxation, it will operate as an income-related program.

The specific level of the tax credit need not be determined now. Benefit levels could be determined by the funds made available through the elimination of other welfare programs. In other words, the funds saved by fully or partially phasing out existing programs could be used to pay for the Graduated Income Supplement.

One virtue of the GIS is that it would absorb, in the reform, programs that are unrelated to need. What the United States now spends on the scores of income-maintenance programs of all kinds would be more than enough to fund the new programs at a level which would totally eliminate poverty.

Because of the gradual rise in tax rates as income increases, a family would not be unduly penalized for each added dollar of earnings. The gradual increase in taxation would insure that there would be no erosion of the work incentive. But, to reiterate, such a result could not be achieved without replacing the

114

Reprinted with permission of John Trever, the *Albuquerque Journal*.

current welfare system with the Graduated Income Supplement...

Everyone on the Same Footing

The Graduated Income Supplement would overcome the principal problem inherent in current welfare programs by providing for universal eligibility. Such a rule would virtually eliminate the potential for abuse.

The annual tax credit would be given to every adult. In addition, an annual tax credit in a lesser amount should go to every child without regard to the composition of any family. Eligibility requirements could thus be completely eliminated.

Under the Graduated Income Supplement, the poor would have to arrange their lives so as to meet such requirements. The computer trainee would not have to quit his job in order to make his family eligible for a subsidized apartment. Fathers would not have to leave home to allow their families to qualify for AFDC. The elderly watchmaker would not be driven to despair by being forced to choose between benefits and work.

In addition, thanks to universal eligibility under the Graduated Income Supplement, the work incentive would be increased among the poor. No longer would a recipient who accepted a job face the prospect of an abrupt loss of benefits. A family would receive the tax credit whether or not it earned income. Under the current AFDC program, family benefits are reduced by the welfare "tax" of 67 percent. Because of the benefit reduction rates, a family may actually lose income when a member goes to work. With the Graduated Income Supplement, whose benefits would be subject to the usual income taxes, people would always find it worth more to work than to stay home and collect benefits.

Elimination of complex eligibility rules would eliminate the need for the tangled welfare bureaucracy and its complicated rules...

Our welfare system is an almost unique combination of the worst elements of government policy: it is wasteful, invites fraud, encourages idleness, and is intolerably expensive. The Graduated Income Supplement is designed to save tax dollars and, at the same time, to achieve the goal of public assistance — providing basic living expenses to the destitute. To implement it would be to repay a debt to ourselves and to the victims of poverty.

"America has to find a way to deal with its human economic failures. Personally I like the Japanese answer."

The "Private Welfare" Alternative

Lester C. Thurow

Lester C. Thurow is Professor of Economics, Massachusetts Institute of Technology. He was a staff economist for the President's Council of Economic Advisors during the Johnson administration. A columnist for *Newsweek* magazine, he has authored several books including *Poverty and Discrimination*, *Investment in Human Capital* and *The Economic Problem*. In the following viewpoint, Mr. Thurow contends that the employer-employee relationship as seen in Japan provides an excellent alternative to the American system — a system which seems to produce an unending chain of "economic misfits."

Consider the following questions while reading:
1. According to Mr. Thurow, what is the Japanese business-man's attitude toward firing a worker?
2. Why does the author believe that firing bad workers is a poor procedure?

Economic security is to modern man what a castle and a moat were to medieval man. Historically the United States has tried to meet the demand for economic security through its social-welfare system. Government helped when misfortunes such as unemployment, old age and illness reduced your market earnings.

The Reagan Administration is now instituting a major reduction in the social safety net. If this is to be other than a temporary trend, the private safety net will have to expand as the public safety net is reduced. If the private safety net is not expanded, voters will quickly turn back to government in pursuit of economic security.

The demand for economic security is not going to disappear. When public-opinion polls ask about desired job characteristics, economic security always takes top place — well above higher pay. Old workers want seniority hiring and firing so that worries about layoffs can be confined to someone else — new workers. Restrictive work rules are designed to provide job security.

Paternal Government

Every group, when it feels its economic security slipping away, runs to government for protection regardless of how loudly it has previously preached the virtues of rugged free enterprise. The list of groups now being given protection is almost endless — autos, steel, textiles, sugar. These groups are not villains. They simply want what each of us wants — economic security. But to meet the demand for economic security with protection is to freeze the economy into sick industries.

The necessary expansion of the private safety net can be seen in Japan — one wealthy industrial country with a much lower level of social-welfare spending. On a recent trip to Japan I became intrigued with the question of at what point a Japanese corporation would fire someone for being an unacceptable worker. Whenever I got a chance I would ask businessmen, large and small, when they had last fired someone and what they would regard as an adequate cause for firing.

Without exception everyone that I talked to said that he had never fired anyone. The reluctance to fire anyone extended from giant corporations with tens of thousands of workers to small corporations with fewer than 150 workers.

In addition to asking about firings I also asked about the existence of workers who simply were not doing their jobs. Every firm I talked to admitted that it had some bad workers who were not performing adequately. They were described in very unflattering terms and, according to company officials, immense social pressure was brought upon them to start

Lester C. Thurow

working. But they were not fired even if they had "not worked in years," largely because management did not entirely blame them for their failures. As the Japanese see it, the entire system somehow shares the blame for inadequate performance: either it has not provided the right job for the individual worker, or it has failed to motivate him properly.

The conversations about these "lazy" workers were very similar to a conversation you might have with a friend who had a son who was an economic failure. The parents are desperately trying to find some way to reform the son, but they also have a sense that they somehow failed to bring him up "right." But whatever the son does and whoever he is, he is still a part of the family. He will not be thrown out.

Society's Duty

Although American firms quickly fire bad workers, there is a problem with that procedure. The offending individual can be thrown out of any one firm, but he cannot be thrown out of society. He is going to exist in our society as long as we are not willing to tolerate starvation on the streets.

How does society deal with individuals who are objectively unemployable? The traditional American answer is to let government welfare bureaucracies deal with the problem. The traditional Japanese answer is to force each private bureaucracy to deal with its share of the problem. The American answer leads to large agglomerations of economic misfits. The Japanese answer prevents any large agglomerations of economic misfits from emerging as a social problem. The economic misfits still exist, but they are supported in the private economy.

America has to find a way to deal with its human economic failures. Personally I like the Japanese answer better than the American answer.

Recognizing Statements That Are Provable

From various sources of information we are constantly confronted with statements and generalizations about social and moral problems. In order to think clearly about these problems, it is useful if one can make a basic distinction between statements for which evidence can be found and other statements which cannot be verified or proved because evidence is not available, or the issue is so controversial that it cannot be definitely proved.

Readers should constantly be aware that magazines, newspapers and other sources often contain statements of a controversial nature. The following activity is designed to allow experimenation with statements that are provable and those that are not.

Most of the following statements are taken from the viewpoints in this chapter. The rest are taken from other sources. Consider each statement carefully. *Mark P for any statement you believe is provable. Mark U for any statement you feel is unprovable because of the lack of evidence. Mark C for statements you think are too controversial to be proved to everyone's satisfaction.*

If you are doing this activity as the member of a class or group, compare your answers with those of other class or group members. Be able to defend your answers. You may discover that others will come to different conclusions than you. Listening to the reasons others present for their answers may give you valuable insights in recognizing statements that are provable.

If you are reading this book alone, ask others if they agree with your answers. You too will find this interaction valuable.

P = *provable*
U = *unprovable*
C = *too controversial*

1. The welfare system of the U.S. is a mess.

2. Under current welfare programs, money is not always received by those who actually need it.

3. In order to reduce the costs of welfare and to make the welfare program achieve its goals, the best alternative would seem to be that of the negative income tax.

4. The one element that saves the present welfare system from being an utter disaster is precisely the red tape and the stigma involved in going on welfare.

5. The various schemes for a guaranteed annual income are no genuine replacement for the universally acknowledged evils of the welfare system.

6. America's welfare system has not abolished poverty, and it has actually led to increased dependency.

7. Despite the risks and perils, an effort must be made to replace welfare as we know it, before the present dependency system completely destroys the work incentive in our country.

8. The Graduated Income Supplement would overcome the principal problem inherent in current welfare programs by providing for universal eligibility.

9. With the Graduated Income Supplement, people would always find it worth more to work than to stay home and collect benefits.

10. The demand for economic security is not going to disappear.

11. Every group, when it feels its economic security slipping away, runs to government for protection.

12. How does society deal with individuals who are objectively unemployable? The traditional American answer is to let government welfare bureaucracies deal with the problem.

13. Because of human nature, all welfare alternatives would eventually degenerate into the current welfare mess.

14. Mandatory government work projects would virtually eliminate unemployment.

Bibliography

The following list of periodical articles deals with the subject matter of this chapter.

Yale Brozen — "Government and the Rich," *National Review*, July 9, 1982, p. 820.

Robert Carleson & Kevin Hopkins vs. George McGovern — "Whose Responsibility is Social Responsibility?" *Public Welfare*, Fall, 1981, p. 8.

Congressional Digest — "Controversy Over the Food Stamp Program," January, 1981.

William J. Coyne — "Isn't It Time to Halt Welfare for the Wealthy?," *USA Today*, July 1982, p. 61.

Anna Dillenberg — "Welfarism," *The Freeman*, November, 1979, p. 675.

Dollars & Sense — "Workfare: An Offer You Can't Refuse," February, 1982, p. 6.

Milton Friedman — "Newsweek on Poverty," *Newsweek*, April 19, 1982, p. 80.

H. J. Gans — "Poverty: What Can Be Done About It?," *Current*, March/April, 1981, p. 16.

George Gilder — "Why I Am Not a Neo-Conservative," *National Review*, March 5, 1982, p. 218.

Henry Hazlitt — "The Case for the Minimal State," *The Freeman*, November, 1979, p. 665.

Peter C. Kratcoski — "Why Work?," *USA Today*, September, 1981, p. 70.

Robert A. Moffitt — "The Negative Income Tax: Would It Discourage Work?," *Monthly Labor Review*, April, 1981, p. 23.

The Progressive — "Welfare Reform 'Forever'," September, 1981, p. 11.

Jack P. Rawlins — "The Fair Society Fantasy," *Newsweek*, March 15, 1982, p. 11.

Time — "Putting the Poor to Work," March 23, 1981, p. 10.

Kenneth Y. Tomlinson — "We Can Clean Up the Welfare Mess," *The Reader's Digest*, April, 1980, p. 82.

Appendix of Organizations

American Association of Retired Persons
1909 K Street N.W.
Washington, DC 20049
(202) 872-4700

Founded in 1958, the association has over 11 million members above the age of 55. The association works to improve every aspect of living for older persons. Publications include *News Bulletin* (monthly) and *Modern Maturity* (bimonthly).

American Public Welfare Association
1125 15th Street N.W. Suite 300
Washington, DC 20005
(202) 293-7550

An association of public welfare agencies, their professional staff members and others interested in public welfare. Founded in 1930, the association publishes 40 to 50 "W-Memo's" per year, 10 *Washington Report*'s per year, the quarterly *Public Welfare* and the weekly *Congressional Record Index*.

Center on Social Welfare Policy and Law
95 Madison Avenue
New York, NY 10016
(212) 679-3709

Founded in 1965, the center brings landmark cases in welfare law and develops materials for welfare rights groups. The center publishes the weekly *Library Bulletin*.

Employee Benefit Research Institute
1800 M Street N.W. Suite 275-N
Washington, DC 20036
(202) 659-0670

An organization of banks, corporations, insurance companies and others interested in the future of employee benefit programs. The institute was organized in 1978 to contribute to the development of effective and responsible public policy in the field through research, publications and education. Publications include the book *Should Pension Assets Be Managed for Social/Political Purposes?* as well as educational pamphlets and research monographs.

Foundation For Economic Education
30 S. Broadway
Irvington, NY 10533
(914) 591-7230

Organized in 1946, the foundation sponsors research on economic studies and promotes private ownership and limited government. Publications include *The Freeman* (monthly) as well as books and pamphlets.

International Council on Social Welfare
Koestlergasse 1/29
A-1060 Vienna, Austria

A coalition of eighty national committees and twenty-eight international organizations, the council was founded in 1928 to promote international cooperation in the field of social welfare. The council conducts study and research and provides information and referral services to members on matters affecting social welfare. English publications include *International Newsletter* (quarterly) and *International Social Work* (quarterly).

International Social Security Association
Case Postale No. 1
CH-1211 Geneva 22, Switzerland

This association of social security administrations, founded in 1927, organizes international technical meetings, conducts research and provides for the exchange of information and assistance. English publications include *International Social Security Review* (quarterly), *Current Research in Social Security* (semi-annual) and irregular technical reports on various problems of social security.

National Association of Social Workers
1425 H Street N.W.   Suite 600
Washington, DC 20005
(202) 628-6800

An organization of professionals and students working or studying in the field of social work. Founded in 1955, the association promotes the quality and effectiveness of social work, sets professional standards and conducts study and research. Publications include *Advocate for Human Services* (biweekly), *Social Work Research and Abstracts* (quarterly) and various books and pamphlets.

National Conference on Social Welfare
1730 M Street N.W.   Suite 911
Washington, DC 20036
(202) 785-0817

This organization of professional and lay persons interested in social welfare and human services was founded in 1873 and conducts annual forums to study basic social welfare problems and issues. Publishes *Bulletin* (quarterly) and *Social Welfare Forum* (annual).

Salvation Army
120 W. 14th Street
New York, NY 10011
(212) 620-4908

An international religious and charitable movement, founded in 1880, dedicated to meeting the physical, spiritual and emotional needs of mankind. Publications include the weekly *The War Cry* and the monthly *SAY*.

Social Legislation Information Service
1346 Connecticut Avenue N.W.
Washington, DC 20036
(202) 223-2396

Founded in 1944, the service publishes bulletins and documents reporting "impartially" on federal social legislation and activities in health, education, welfare, housing and employment. Publishes *Washington Legislation Bulletin* (semi-monthly).

Social Welfare History Group
c/o Philip Popple
School of Social Work
University of Tennessee
P.O. Box 90440
Nashville, TN 37209
(615) 329-1212

This organization of historians, social workers and others interested in research, teaching and preservation of historical records of social welfare was founded in 1956. Publications include *Newsletter* published three times a year.

Volunteers of America
340 W. 85th Street
New York, NY 10024
(212) 873-2600

A religious social welfare organization, founded in 1896, to give spiritual and material aid to those in need. Publishes the monthly *The Volunteer*.

The Editor

David L. Bender is a history graduate from the University of Minnesota. He also has an M.A. in government from St. Mary's University in San Antonio, Texas. He has taught social problems at the high school level for several years. He is the general editor of the *Opposing Viewpoints Series* and has authored many of the titles in the series.